MEN BUILT FOR OTHERS
Life Lessons from Those Serving Life Sentences

Compiled by: Ted Gray,
Richard Mireles, Jason Bryant,
and Matthew Braden

Edited by:
Kail Cohen

Foreword by: Farshad Asl
Bestselling Author of *"No Excuses" Mindset*

**Men Built For Others:
Life Lessons from Those Serving Life Sentences**

Copyright © 2018 Top Leaders Publishing Inc.
P.O Box 33272
Granada Hills CA 91394

All Rights Reserved.

ISBN: 978-1-64184-019-4 (hardback)
ISBN: 978-1-64184-039-2 (paperback)
ISBN: 978-1-64184-020-0 (ebook)

All rights reserved. No part of this book may be reproduced or transmitted in any form or by any means, electronic, or mechanical, including photocopying or recording, or by an information storage and retrieval system, without permission in writing by the author.

All translations of this work must be approved in writing by the author. Please contact our publisher for permission to translate and distribution agreements. Printed in the United States of America.

To order more copies for your team, please visit our website at www.topleaders.com or contact us at (310) 872-8328.

First Edition

Dedicated to all those who've ever felt lost and insignificant, *Men Built for Others* conveys your story. It's for those who've made wrong choices and felt condemned to a life of painful and indescribable regret. However, through God's help and guidance, transformed their lives, committed to working with a life coach, and found their way and purpose toward positively impacting the lives of others.

Contents

Acknowledgements		vii
Foreword		xi
Letter from a Friend		xv
Preface		xvii
Introduction		xxi
1	You Can't Give What You Don't Have	1
2	Worry About What God Thinks	13
3	There's Nothing Worse than Being Unable to Tell Your Own Story	25
4	Life is About Moments and Relationships	39
5	Intentionality Paves the Way to Success	49
6	Everything Worth Living for is Worth Fighting For	63
7	You're Either Making the World Better or Worse	75
8	The Least Among You Shall be the Greatest	85
9	Serving God by Being of Service to Others	101
10	Existence is Justified by Life; Life is Defined by Service	113
11	Why Pay Someone When You Can Do it for Free?	133
Afterword		151
About the Primary Contributors		157

Acknowledgements

Thank you to Farshad Asl for lighting the proverbial fire and encouraging us to think outside of the box.

Thank you to Roger Nielsen for equipping us with resources and reminding us that greatness cannot be locked up.

Thank you to Eugene Dey and Jesse Bonderman for being Men Built for Others.

Thank you to the Crop Organization, specifically Mitch Gray, for investing in us and believing in the mission.

Thank you to our families for loving us in spite of the poor decisions we made in our past and supporting us in the vision that we have for our futures.

Our Collective and Sincere Thanks...

We'd like to collectively extend our special appreciation and acknowledgment to all those who contributed to the overall compilation and process of writing this incredible book and labor of love.

We're indebted to those who transformed our modest hopes into tangible dreams while serving time in prison.

This body of work wouldn't have been possible had it not been for the many tireless individuals who overcame their long-held fears, demons and deep-rooted shame to vulnerably share their personal accounts of powerful transformation because of His will.

To our fellow inmates, we thank you for sharing your stories; even if they didn't make it into this book. We thank all the translators and editors who gave so much of themselves to make this book what it is today.

We're grateful for the never-ending support and gracefulness of Chaplin B.D. Min.

We're also profoundly grateful for the professional editing and detail work done by Kail Cohen.

We certainly appreciate the design work created by Walter Rivas.

Men Built for Others is evidence that "faith" and "teamwork," unlike our physical bodies, can never be restrained or locked up. There's always time to transform your life and live with a no-excuses mindset. Take charge of your circumstances regardless of what they may be before they take charge and ownership of your fate.

Foreword

This exceptional book is composed of a series of transformational and deeply inspiring true stories. It was written, edited, and compiled by men who learned from their past mistakes and became laser-focused on rebuilding their futures with brilliant hope, unshakeable faith, and great determination.

"We're all sinners, but some of us got caught." Those were the first words I spoke when addressing inmates at the Correctional Training Facility, located in Soledad, California. It was part of the graduation speech I delivered.

When my dear friend, Roger Nielsen (a servant leader whose life was also transformed while incarcerated), invited me to the prison graduation, I was excited and nervous. After all, I had never been inside a prison and didn't know what to expect, how to connect with the inmates, or even where to start for that matter. On many levels, I knew this would be one of the most important speeches I'd ever deliver. I prayed and asked God to lead me towards a path that would allow me to add value to the lives of all who'd be in attendance.

Despite it being my first experience visiting a prison, I knew it wouldn't be the last. I was genuinely impressed by the energy, passion, and excitement of these men. I recall watching them worship before their graduation ceremony. Because of how beautifully they were singing, I swear for a moment, it felt like I was in heaven. Immediately I realized one could find and experience happiness wherever they are in life.

After delivering my speech on transformational leadership, I spent hours more at the prison. While in the visiting room, I met two of the prison's most well-known and influential leaders, Ted Gray and Richard Mireles. God's divine intervention led me to introduce myself. Immediately I knew to inquire whether these men knew they could impact change and make a difference in people's lives even while incarcerated.

"How can we?" they replied.

"How many inmates are there in this correctional center?" I asked.

"Over 5,000."

"How many inmates do you think you can find who've transformed their lives while incarcerated?"

I encouraged the men to build a team of leaders in charge of selecting, collecting, and drafting the stories describing how their lives had been transformed.

God opened my heart to engage with these men intentionally. Because of His will, we now have this book. Even though I knew the personal stories and details of the eleven men whose stories are featured, my eyes were filled with tears after reading this book's first draft.

It wasn't easy for any of these men to share the consequences of their wrongdoing and poor judgment for the entire world to see. However, because they have done so, they've earned my utmost respect. Further, I am truly inspired by their courage and vulnerability in ways that I've never previously experienced.

God is always present in our lives even though we may feel alone. Throughout all of the success and failures of my life, I know that God's plan has always been for me to help others. There's been no other project more fulfilling or rewarding in my life than mentoring and guiding these Men Built for Others.

All praise is due to God for uniting my path in friendship with Roger Nielsen, Richard Mireles, and Ted Gray. I am indebted to all of you for inviting me to play a small part in your extraordinary journey of becoming Men Built for Others.

This book has the power to change lives. Are you're searching for internal peace? Are you struggling to overcome destructive habits? Are you trying to help a loved one when hope feels lost? Use this book as your resource and instrument for change.

> *I know that my Redeemer lives!*
> *What joy this blest assurance gives!*
> *He lives, he lives, who once was dead;*
> *He lives, my everlasting head!*
>
> *He lives to bless me with his love;*
> *He lives to plead for me above;*
> *He lives my hungry soul to feed;*
> *He lives to help in time of need.*
>
> *He lives and grants me daily breath;*
> *He lives, and I shall conquer death;*
> *He lives my mansion to prepare;*
> *He lives to bring me safely there.*
>
> *He lives, all glory to his name!*
> *He lives, my Savior, still the same;*
> *What joy this blest assurance gives:*
> *I know that my Redeemer lives! Amen*
>
> - Samuel Medley

Farshad Asl - Entrepreneur, Regional Director of Bankers Life, Founder of Top Leaders, Inc., Certified John Maxwell Leadership Coach, Teacher, International Speaker, and Amazon Bestselling Author of *The No Excuses Mindset: A Life of Purpose, Passion, and Clarity.*

A Message From A Friend:
An Insider's Perspective from the Outside World

Nearly two decades ago, Richard Mireles and I were cellmates at Soledad State Prison, the inspiration for these eleven stories and the birthplace of *Men Built for Others*.

I don't know how to sufficiently convey my unwavering respect and appreciation for my friends: Richard Mireles and Ted Gray. Therefore, I'll just say—they're the real deal!

Richard and Ted, have singlehandedly stirred the hearts and minds of countless individuals within the confines of Soledad and outside the prison walls too. Their gift of friendship has profoundly impacted my life and transformed me into the man I am today.

In 2001, while incarcerated, I had a life-changing conversation with Richard. While we were walking the loop of the prison's recreation area, I felt compelled to share Theodore Roosevelt's famous quote: "Nobody cares how much you know, until they know how much you care."

Richard is one of the smartest men I've ever known. However, he hasn't always cared about other people—to be entirely transparent. Sharing that quote with Richard, in many distinct ways set him on fire. This book is the result of Richard being a Man Built for Others.

Richard became more sociable and eventually introduced me to Ted Gray. Ted is a forward-thinker and an undeniable trailblazer. He stretches himself and everyone else around him to strive to do the right thing and to become the best version of themselves. Ted embodies tenacity and grit more than anyone else I've known.

Several years later I was paroled. I then had the honor of asking my dear friend Farshad Asl, to speak at the prison's graduation ceremony.

After delivering a remarkably inspiring call-to-action graduation speech, Farshad challenged Richard and Ted to consider how they could impact change outside the prison walls. Farshad taught them how to embrace a no-excuses mindset so they could obtain and research stories which served as the foundation for what I know is one the rawest, most vulnerable and powerful books on the market.

I'll never forget witnessing the surge of hope that came over my friends' faces after listening to Farshad's uplifting words.Hearing someone from the outside world honestly say, "I believe in you," was the catalyst for them achieving greatness.

Richard and Ted appreciated the fact they'd have to enlist the help of others if there would ever be a book. So they collaborated with two of Ted's best friends—Jason Bryant and Matthew Braden. They each brought unique skills and distinct perspectives to this project.

Aside from being present for the birth of my own kids, I've never experienced such pride as witnessing the transformation of ALL the men who dedicated themselves to writing this book.

I encourage you to read our book with a sincerely open heart and mind. And to the extent that you can, please do so with suspension of any judgment.

Roger Nielsen—Entrepreneur, Certified John Maxwell Leadership Coach, Teacher, Speaker, and author of *Greatness Cannot Be Locked Up*

Preface

"Virtue is a state of war, and to live in it we have always to combat with ourselves."

- Jean-Jacques Rousseau

This is not a book that celebrates or glamorizes the criminal underworld. In fact, it is our goal to expose the nefarious prison subculture for what it truly is—a lie and excuse to live a life with low expectations. The prevailing culture of California's prison system invites men to collude in expecting the worst from one another and then rewards their antisocial attitudes and behaviors. Yet, even within such an antisocial environment, when willing to look, one will find revolutionary pockets; counter culture islands of transformation where men choose to support the best in each other. For example, instead of expecting someone to "put in work" (prison vernacular for perpetrating violence), responsible men are expected to honor their higher commitments, which normally includes living out their faith, living with integrity, or simply being a good son, brother, father, husband, or friend. Instead of being expected to use drugs, inflict harm on others, or participate in other criminal activities, responsible men are expected to earn a GED, obtain a vocational trade, or pursue a college degree.

This book is about a cohort of men at California's Correctional Training Facility in Soledad State Prison who are not only part of this culture of transformation but are also each responsible for the growing revolution. They have planted a flag for something worthwhile, new, and unprecedented. Like Martin Luther, the Protestant Reformer, they have taken a stand for the reformation of themselves as well as the prison culture. Because of this commitment, the island is growing and other men are beginning to want what they have—the freedom to transcend their circumstances, to make choices according to their core values, and a future worth having—instead of simply adhering to the criminal norms of prison.

While this book was written by prisoners, it's for anyone and everyone. We say this with conviction because we believe that anyone can find value in the transformational stories of these men. However, for those of you who have ever felt as if there is no hope for a new and unprecedented future, or that you have no choice but to live a life of compromise because of your circumstances, then this book is especially for you.

In the following pages, you will meet men, including the editors, who have committed terrible crimes and have justly served several years in prison—some of them, two or three decades worth. During their incarceration, most of the men have wrestled with, and even considered surrendering to despair. Instead, they found purpose for their lives. They have discovered a transcendent cause and have committed themselves to something bigger than themselves, and as a result, they have become Men Built for Others. They are our fellow soldiers of a cultural revolution; they are our fellow workers in restorative justice, and most importantly, they are our friends and brothers.

It must be said that the insight contained within this book has come at a terrible cost to the people we harmed, which includes not just the direct victims of our crimes, but also their families, law enforcement agencies, our communities, and even our own families. We understand that the fruit of true remorse is a transformed life. Therefore, we hope that readers walk away from the following stories not only having experienced that each writer has owned responsibility for his past actions, beliefs, values, and attitudes, but that he is also now living the life of a Man Built for Others as a natural expression of his remorse.

Primary Contributors

Introduction

> *"Men need to bring men in. Men need to stand for other men. Men need to rescue the men who are adrift. Men need the presence of other valiant men—both living and dead—to draw them out to be what they are meant to be."*
>
> - Stephen Mansfield

"Take off your clothes and throw them in the bin . . . now show me your hands . . . raise your arms . . . open your mouth . . . turn around . . . show me the bottoms of your feet . . . now squat and cough three times." This is the anthem that all inmates are greeted with upon their woeful arrival at a California Department of Corrections and Rehabilitation (CDCR) reception center. The institution's drab walls and razor-wire fences reflect a spiritless atmosphere of control and mechanical efficiency that serves as a stark reminder that one's freedom has been surrendered.

After this first of many such "dances" that will be conducted in the interest of "safety and security," a stoic correctional officer will pose one simple question: "Who do you run with?" This question is the crude product of an inmate-imposed segregation, which the CDCR has honed as a tool for conflict management. This question is the lifeblood of an insidious system of antisocial rules that govern how thousands of people with different-colored skin (or contrasting gang affiliations) will interact within a few shared acres of land. This question is the standard by which unrepentant prisoners can justify their criminality and perpetuate their irresponsibility.

Established by convicts from decades past, and dogmatically followed by those who lack the vision to consider new possibilities, these rules leave the air of most prison yards thick with a texture of suspicion, anger, hostility, and despair. Sadly, for those who give themselves over to this atmosphere, there is a very real experience of having no choice in their day-to-day survival. Their low expectations for living a purposeful life is the result of their resignation to "How it is." Unbeknownst to these prison creatures; however, is that their perceived lack of choice is in itself a decision that they have made.

In December of 1999, my best friend (Ted) and I (Jason) made the worst decision of our short lives as we committed a horrific crime that resulted in the murder of a man, the devastation of several families, the horror of our community, and each of us receiving life-terms in prison. Ted was a 22-year-old White man, I was a 20-year-old Black man, and together we entered a prison culture that did not look kindly upon interracial codefendants. While housed at one of the most notorious prisons in California, Ted and I spent seven years walking the same yards together, but never really being "together." The fact that we went to high school together, played sports together, and shared fond memories together, did not matter. The reality that he lived with me and my parents for a time, went with us on trips to amusement parks, and enjoyed holiday meals with our family, was irrelevant. The history of me serving as a best man at his wedding, being like an uncle to his two sons, and the fact that I viewed him as the only brother I ever had, threatened dangerous consequence. Both of us accepted the status quo that Blacks and Whites were enemies . . . we succumbed to the lie of that's "How it is" in prison.

Ted and I took different paths during those early years of our incarceration. Having a lengthier sentence than me, Ted decided that by engaging in prison politics, he could have some say in "How it is" and avoid being used by others. I, on the other hand, decided to immerse myself in education as a way to avoid the powerful pull from gangs, but I also remained carefully observant to the rules of "How it is." Both of us decided that it was more important to respect those antisocial rules than to honor our friendship. As a result, we minimized our encounters to a head nod here, or a few short words there, as we crossed paths each day on a small lot of land.

It wasn't until 2010 that Ted and I would find the courage to begin breaking through the toxic prison perspective of "How it is." Both of us had demonstrated enough good behavior to warrant our transfer to a lower security prison. I arrived at CTF-Soledad in 2009, and providentially, Ted arrived at the same prison a year later. When I first saw Ted on the yard, I experienced a conflict of emotions. I felt nostalgic and happy at seeing my childhood friend, but I was also uncertain and cautious about his motivations. Had the years of living under oppressive, antisocial prison politics changed him forever? Were there any vestiges left of the young man whom I once called my brother as we sat at my family's table and ate Thanksgiving dinner? Fortunately, the answer was not only that my brother had remained himself, but something new had developed that I had never seen in him before. Ted had undergone a transformation in his thinking as he discovered an insatiable desire to add value to the prison culture (and the community) in substantial ways. During this transformation, he was guided to Christ by his Christian friend Richard Mireles. Then, after we met Matthew Braden, who is an irreplaceable member of our team and a vital contributor to our shared work, we created a think tank called: "Inside Solutions," to support a vision that would transform the culture of prison.

For the last seven years, Ted and I have been nearly inseparable. Together, along with Rich and Matt, we have worked tirelessly to address our personal issues, create programs that give back to the community (in prison and out), and facilitate conversations that matter for the people who need them the most. We have found and enrolled other men with remarkable commitment from different backgrounds to spread the word about the lie of "How it is" and fan the transformative flame of "How it could be." Of personal importance, Ted and I have redefined what it means to be friends. In our criminality, we wrongly believed that friendship meant blind loyalty. What we have come to learn and appreciate through this experience is that true friendship means being committed to the most important things in each others' lives. This means that today we stand for one another's commitment to God, to our families, and to being of service to others.

Our Inside Solutions team has benefited from the talents of numerous prolific thinkers, visionaries, collaborators, and scrupulously committed workers, many of whom have contributed to this manuscript. Ted, Rich, Matt, and I typify what the old adherents to "How it is" would consider an "odd team." Living within an environment where people with different skin color or criminal factions are clearly divided by lines of neatly manicured plots of grass, it is exceedingly uncommon to see two Whites, a Black, and a Hispanic walking the track together, laughing together, eating together, and planning a future together.

While these types of ethnically integrated friendships do exist to lesser degrees within prison walls, make no mistake that it is greatly disdained by those antisocial elements that influence the general context of a prison. That being said, our entire team made a decision that in spite of the tension, we would honor our brotherhood by standing with each other in our higher commitments while working together to affect change within our community.

The stories within these pages mark the inception of a revolution to upheave "How it is." What follows are the narratives of men who have committed heinous acts of violence and tyranny within their communities. This reality must be stated openly because each man's story is rooted in discoveries that were made after a tragic fall. Each fall is marked by specifically shameful deeds that delivered unique hurt and grief to their respective victims . . . a reality that cannot and must not be overshadowed by any value derived from this work of repentance.

Keeping these lamentable truths in mind, the experiences shared within this volume each represent a migration away from the criminal status quo. Some of these discoveries took time as men slowly came to realize that the life they had been living was not a life at all, but rather, something more like a predictable death march to the beat of a drum that was not their own. Others experienced a more sudden awakening as the harsh veneer of institutional protocol jolted them into a piercing awareness of the blessings that they had forfeited. And some, through God's grace, arrived at the decision to change as they grasped at a vestige of their faith from a heroin-induced coma. Despite the amount of time served, the type of experience lived, or test of tribulation endured, each of the men whose testimonies line these pages has undergone a remarkable transformation.

That being said, some vital features should be mentioned regarding the perspective of transformation as we are presenting it to you, the reader. While each contributor's story provides the contour of an eventual change in their outward behavior, their very outlook on life has undergone a quantum shift to something brand new . . . it has transformed. This newness serves as the nucleus of these men's lives today and is the catalyst for a cultural revolution that has flourished into a prosocial island of transformation. This realization is unprecedented in their experience—as it was something that had never before been considered, and it opened their eyes to a future that is both actionable and worth having.

Over the course of seven years, the entire Inside Solutions team has worked hard to keep this promise, and in the process, we have reached some remarkable milestones. From creating and successfully launching an Alcohol and Other Drugs (AOD) counseling certification program (which now has 30 state certified AOD inmate counselors), to delivering scores of transformational leadership seminars to prisoners, college students, and college administrators, our team has toiled steadily to impact change. When our lead counselors were awarded with certificates of Senatorial Recognition for Inside Solutions' work in the recovery community, the warden of the institution remarked, "Inmates don't get things like this." He was right. Our calling to contribute, and our commitment to each other, had produced truly unprecedented outcomes . . . but that was just the beginning.

The purpose of mentioning Inside Solutions' achievements is to highlight the possibilities that can blossom from the seeds of transformation and commitment. Our team is comprised of goal-oriented individuals, but if you were to ask us about our most cherished accomplishment, we would answer, "The stories of the men within this book." With that being said, we must emphasize that these personal discoveries are the sole proprietorship of the men who chose something new for their lives. Our part, however small, has been to stand with them in their new commitments and provide them with a platform to share their transformations in a meaningful way.

The work that we have pledged ourselves to is the work of possibility and the work of relationships. It was the work of exploring new possibilities that awoke the power of transformation in our own lives. As each of us took off the proverbial blinders of "How it is," we discovered an entire world of new possibilities and untapped resources that we had never before considered. As we began scrutinizing the results of our worn out worldviews, we began to experience the freedom to create a new space for thinking in terms of the unprecedented.

This book is overflowing with stories of the unprecedented. From deep within the confines of what many would suggest is the most oppressive environment in our nation, these men have unearthed a brand of liberty that cannot be cheapened by clichés about the freedom of one's mind. No, these men have learned a new way to live each moment with appreciation, to think with unlimited possibilities, to own their choices with sober responsibility, and above all, to stand with authentic commitment for serving others in a way that moves them closer to the future they envision for themselves.

Perhaps it is true that something must be lost before it can be found. For these men, that has certainly been the case. After making one, two, and in some cases an entire series of destructive choices, these prisoners made a powerful shift that transformed the way in which they relate to their very lives. It is our sincere hope that the epiphanies which the contributors to this book have discerned in their own lives might serve as a type of inspiration for the reader. We, the Inside Solutions' team, fervently believe that the transformation which these men have experienced while encapsulated within a hate-filled tomb can provide anyone with a valuable resource for living with empowerment. We trust this to be true because before any of these men made the choice to commit their crimes—they were sons, brothers, fathers, and most importantly, people just like you.

The parallel in our shared humanity is drawn because if such profound transformation can be discovered for men within a vacuum of hopelessness, an environment designed to breed despair, then what future might become possible for you out there? The answer is a true paradox because while the possibilities for your life are indeed limitless, only you can discover and actualize those possibilities. If you are experiencing being stuck, or in some way limited by your circumstances, we hope that the stories within this book will inspire you to be courageous, to choose a clear vision for something new, and to discover the unprecedented.

Men Built for Others Profile

Name: Chris Wachniuk
Date of Birth: 11/10/73
Sentence: 25 years-to-life
Parole Eligibility: 2018

Leadership Maxim: *You can't give what you don't have.*
Person He Is Most Inspired By: His grandfather, Weston Smith
Favorite Book: *Conquistadors of the Useless* by Lionel Terray

Education & Interests
- Associate of Arts in Behavioral Science
- Internationally Certified Alcohol and Drug Counselor II (ICADC-II)

More than anyone else that we know in prison, Chris is the person who is most committed to advancing the mission of recovery and sobriety. He was instrumental in developing and delivering the first three-day recovery conference ever held within a state prison. Chris mentors dozens of prisoners in maintaining their commitment to sobriety and has recently celebrated his tenth year of being drug and alcohol free. He is a leader within Soledad's Christian community, and lives his life as a Man Built for Others.

Chapter 1

There comes a time when you have to leave all that is familiar and go on into the unknown with God.

- John Eldredge

Imagine the view of an artistic masterpiece from only a few inches away—its color, texture, and contrasts. The painting could be nearly overwhelming as the viewer examines each fine detail with intensity. Yet, what might be missed when the perspective is held at such close proximity? Is that how the master desired his audience to interact with his creation? Even with the beauty of the close and intimate, there is so much lost when the grander experience is never viewed. When viewing a Jackson Pollock from an inch away, hearing one note of a Beethoven symphony, or reading a single line from Maya Angelou, perspective is lost and the grand design is never experienced in fullness.

It is tempting, and I think quite natural, to focus on the close and isolated perspective of our individual experiences. There is a discipline required in taking a reflective step back from life and viewing the bigger picture. As I'm writing this, I am aware of the separate experiences I've had that have shaped me and been influential in my life: the loss of my father, the end of a romantic relationship, the challenge of getting sober, and serving a life sentence in prison. To take any one of those examples and describe a single moment of transformation doesn't seem all that challenging; yet, each of those are only a small stroke of the brush on the canvas of my life. Each of those experiences, each of those brush strokes, contributes to the larger picture. Without the contribution of each individual experience, there would be no greater whole.

In each of my experiences, I have grown to appreciate and value the process of these events and to find the purpose as each experience builds the grand design. None of this is constant, though. I find value and purpose, but not nearly as quickly as I would like. There are many moments of transformation that all contribute to a lifelong process of metamorphosis—sometimes quickly, sometimes slowly.

As I share a particular experience of significance in the following pages, I am again reflecting on the purpose of God as He works out the seemingly small and trivial circumstances for His grand design. How easily I forget that He is the Master Painter, the Composer, the Great Poet; I get the privilege to be His canvas, or better yet, a small piece of His canvas in His amazing program. While reading the following experience, my encouragement is to view it through the lens of Proverbs 17:3, which states, "The crucible is for silver, and the furnace is for gold, and the LORD tests hearts." The circumstances of our lives are opportunities to be established, refined, and ultimately to honor God through His process. Here is one of those opportunities from my life.

The sun seemed to burn my skin and blind my eyes as I stepped outside and into daylight for the first time after a ten-month lockdown. No handcuffs, no shackles and chains, no correctional officer to escort me. My thoughts reeled and spun as I walked across the prison yard, "How would others view me? Am I going to get jumped? Will I live through this?" Nothing in my life was the same. Ten months of confinement with no outside contact had been the fire of refinement as I walked away from my past and cut ties with my previous lifestyle. Now came the testing; now came the moment of truth. And now came the question: Had my crucible been authentic?

I had spent the majority of my life hiding from my fear of rejection and seeking easy, quick 'fixes' to fill the deep loneliness I felt. I started using drugs and alcohol when I was fifteen, and I had been in a relentless pursuit to feel accepted by others and control my environment from an early age. I created a belief system for myself that connected my value as a person to what I imagined others thought of me. For as far back as I can remember, I was thoroughly committed to this ideal – *get approval at any cost*. Of course, I never realized this was my thinking as a child, an adolescent, or even as a young adult. It seemed to be the natural progression of my thinking that I would act out as the class clown, followed by ditching class to smoke cigarettes, and then marijuana. It was not long before I was sneaking out of the house to drink and spend the nights with girls. All of this was directly related to what I thought would impress others; it was an easy way to make 'friends.' All the while my thinking was becoming more and more irresponsible. I vandalized my neighborhood, stole from my community, and began to act out violently. By the time I finished high school I had been arrested several times, been to rehab and a group home three times, and was quickly headed toward a lifetime of jails, institutions, and destruction. This was how I lived; it was the lens through which I experienced life.

My involvement in a murder in 1996 is the logical outcome of my thinking and behavior. I used others to feel better about myself; but it was never for good, or with a willingness to sacrifice what I viewed as my survival. I had dedicated myself to shortcuts and easy paths. Prison was no exception. In fact, it was the perfect environment for me to use drugs and alcohol, act out violently, and manipulate others. Not only was I physically imprisoned, but I had created a system of thinking that was far more restrictive than any wall or fence—and much more destructive. My entire life remained anchored to that same idea, *get approval at any cost.*

Although I had known this way of thinking was wrong, I was unwilling to examine myself and consider anything new. However, in September of 2006, the pain of staying the same began to outweigh the fear of changing. For the first time in my life, I genuinely sought after sobriety and made a decision to go to any length in order to stay sober and grow spiritually. My journey began as a bumpy road with several hiccups and poor choices. In 2007, I relapsed and struggled to distance myself from the phony reputation I had built as a prison tough guy. After recovering from my relapse, I kept my commitment to abstain from drinking or using drugs. This enabled me to grow, to draw closer to God, to build a set of principles, and develop character. For the very first time in my life, I began to discover who I was and the value of others. I was not perfect by any means, but I had begun to move in a positive direction. There were small victories and challenges nearly every day, but it would be two years later that I would face one of the greatest moments in my life.

I had been sober for nearly two years in August of 2008 when this ten-month lockdown began. Somehow, though, this morning seemed to have an ominous feel to it. I would later learn that over a hundred inmates housed in a dorm on the facility where I was living had been involved in a mass race-gang riot in the middle of the night. This was the third incident of its kind in only a few weeks and would be the justification for nearly a year of confinement for several hundred inmates. This was the scene I awoke to that summer morning in August.

Over the next several days, the picture became clear that this would be a long time of confinement with extra strict custody procedures. There would be no outside visits allowed, no phone calls to family, no commissary privileges, and no outside activities. We were to be confined to our six-by-twelve foot cells for twenty-four hours a day. When we left for showers or a doctor's visit we would be handcuffed or shackled. Showers would be offered every seventy-two hours; and we would receive mail after the prison processed it, which took two or three weeks. Confinement and isolation can break a human being, which is often the point. Yet, that same confinement and isolation can also become the fire of refinement if one uses it for that purpose. A prison cell can become the cocoon from which the butterfly emerges transformed into a creature of beauty.

Although I had nearly two years of sobriety from alcohol and drugs, I had straddled the fence when it came to walking away from a position of power and control among other inmates. For several years, I had been involved in 'prison politics' and even though I claimed I wanted to change, I repeatedly gave advice that influenced the outcomes of the politics among White prisoners. It was in the spring of 2008 that I finally made the decision to stop placing myself in those conversations. The process that began in the spring became my crucible of transformation that stretched over the next ten months. The work had begun.

Facing a long time of confinement can be intimidating. It requires a mental discipline and a regimented routine to maintain mental, emotional, spiritual, and physical health. Even then, the toll is enormous on the mind and soul. As the reality set in that we would be in our cells for nearly a year, I chose to spend my time each day reading, writing, exercising, and meditating. Much of my time each day was spent journaling, reading the Bible, and in prayer.

There was nothing new to me about being on lockdown, but the way in which I was going to live through this lockdown would result in a new experience. I decided that I would be very intentional in my conversations with others. During lockdowns, most of the conversations that inmates have with each other are held while they wait to see a doctor in the medical department or through small hand-written notes called kites that are sent from cell to cell. My commitment was that I would not communicate with anyone about prison politics, I would not engage in negative conversations, and I would not write or pass kites. Because of my past involvement in prison politics, the temptation to do these things was often present and strong. These situations challenged me on a daily basis; yet, I experienced a growing sense of accomplishment as I was able to stand in my commitment and follow through.

The pivotal moment came for me in the winter months of 2009. The cellmate I had at the time was a younger guy named Bobby who had recently been released from Administrative Segregation. He wanted to change, but he was still struggling with the challenges of peer pressure and fear. One evening he received a letter from a friend of his who had been housed at another prison. Prisoners create rules and policies that form a code within the system—some are well known and understood, others are vague and unclear. My cellmate's friend had been housed at a prison that was known as a protective custody (PC) prison—the 'rules' dictate against living in one of those prisons. As a result, if that young man came to our prison, he would be attacked for staying at the PC prison. Even though I did not personally care that my cellmate was corresponding with his friend, I knew that others would, and they would enforce their brand of prison justice. So when I explained to Bobby how the rules worked, he looked straight at me and said, "That is my friend. I don't care what the prison politics are. I'll stick up for him. I've known him my whole life. I'll go to the dirt for him." The cell was quiet as I stared at Bobby and nodded my head. I don't remember if I said anything. I know I felt a level of respect for his decision. Those words, "I don't care what the prison politics are. I'll stick up for him," seemed to speak to my soul. How could this young guy have such a conviction? How could he be willing to go against the mores of our prison culture? Something in me knew he was right and that what he was committed to was greater than the fear of following the crowd. He had something I wanted to have in my own life.

For several days I could not free myself of the words that Bobby spoke. As I went through each day's regimen, that conversation clung to my thoughts; there was something valuable there, and I wanted to find it. There is something attractive about someone who is committed to their values and is willing to suffer for what they believe in. I remember thinking how being willing to suffer and being willing to risk what others thought of him was actually a place of freedom in his life. I had been experiencing a level of freedom but not quite like that. I wanted that kind of liberty.

Sometime in the few days after our initial conversation, I recall a powerful and clear thought that occurred to me, "Chris, at what point are you willing to 'go to the dirt' for what you believe?" Bobby had known his friend for most of his life, I had known myself all of my life. When would I be willing to 'suffer' for what I believed was right? In that moment, I became clear on what I was committed to. I was no longer willing to live violently, regardless of the cost. I was no longer willing to even pretend that I would go along with what I did not agree with, whether it be violence, racism, bigotry, or anything else. I was unwilling to live that way another day. In that moment, I became clear about what I was committed to and how I would choose to live.

For the next several months I relied upon this experience as an anchor for who I would be in my life. This was a principle I could use if I was in prison, free, on lockdown, or walking laps on the yard. I was learning how to be a truly free human being. By finding my values, committing to what I believed in, and standing in that commitment, I was being set free.

I would love to say that the next few months were free from fear and challenges and that I began to soar through life in victory. The truth is that I battled with fear of rejection and being attacked for what I stood for. I was often unsure of how I would get through the next several months, let alone years. After four more months of being on lockdown, I was selected as one of the first inmates to be released from confinement.

I was scared and nervous as that first day came and I was allowed to leave my cell. I felt sick to my stomach. The sun seemed to burn my skin and blind my eyes as I stepped into the daylight for the first time in over ten months. No handcuffs, no shackles, no chains, and no correctional officer to escort me. My mind reeled and spun as I walked across the prison yard thinking, "How are the fellas going to view me? Am I going to get jumped? Will I live through this?" Nothing in my life was the same.

For the first time in my life I believed in something that I was willing to suffer for. In the midst of fear and the temptation to run back to what was familiar, I experienced a new freedom for the first time in my life. The beliefs and ideas that I once held had been shaved and ground down through months of isolation and a new faith had taken root—I had a new faith. I would live in each moment as free as any man because I had something to live for. No longer dictated by fear, I was set free to be myself and live. As I walked across the prison yard I felt as though I had wings and could fly.

Sharing that story, I see someone far greater than myself at work. Surely the sovereign hand of God allows and orchestrates the circumstances of our lives for His purpose. As I step back and gain perspective, limited though it may be, I am humbled at the thought of how God shapes and forms a life like mine. I am the little piece of silver in the Refiner's fire—the crucible. And I am reminded that it is not the single experience that is the goal. That is not the end. Each crucible, each cocoon experience, and every stroke of the Painter's brush is a piece of the grand design—the process of being transformed into His masterpiece.

As a result of these refining experiences, I have been given opportunity upon opportunity to step into a purposeful life. As God has brought me out of a lifestyle consumed with self, He has shown me the value of working with others and using my own experiences, both pleasant and painful, as resource to be of service. The amazing truth I am learning is that the Master Painter never wastes a brush stroke—NEVER. Each experience, each crucible, is an opportunity to help someone else who may be journeying a similar path. I have been given these awesome moments to develop and build programs that support healing and rehabilitation in my own life and in the lives of others.

For several years I have been able to work with the editors of this book in addiction treatment projects, leadership development programs, community outreach and building ventures, and multiple Christian programs within our local church. Most recently, I have had the privilege of working with DUI offenders who have been convicted of murder as a result of their DUI offenses. Developing a process group for these men that centers on personal choice and responsibility has been tremendously rewarding as I have been able to witness these men grow and acquire an understanding of their responsibilities and contributions—and then begin to give back and be of service to their communities.

This has become my purpose—to offer to others the possibility of using those most destructive experiences of their lives to reach and love those who are hurting. I certainly have not done this perfectly; however, I am committed to shining light into the darkness of my own life in order to serve others. One of the editors of this book has often asked me this anchoring question, "Chris, are you a leaner, or are you a lifter?" My purpose today is to give, to build-up, to lift, and to not lean or weigh others down. Every moment, every victory, and every seeming defeat is an opportunity to honor God and love others. The apostle Paul wrote, "Blessed be the God and Father of our Lord Jesus Christ, the Father of mercies and God of all comfort, who comforts us in all our affliction, *so that we may be able to comfort those who are in any affliction, with the comfort with which we ourselves are comforted*" (2 Corinthians 1:3, 4 *my emphasis added*). Each crucible experience is an opportunity to love and serve others in the same way I have been loved and cared for. Not a wasted moment; not a wasted brush stroke in the Master's plan.

Men Built for Others Profile

Name: Robert Esquivel
Date of Birth: 7/16/79
Sentence: 48 years-to-life
Parole Eligibility: 2020

Leadership Maxim: *Worry about what God thinks.*
Person He Is Most Inspired By: His mother
Favorite Book: *Man's Search for Meaning* by Viktor Frankl

Education & Interests
- Associate of Arts in Liberal Arts
- Associate of Science in General Studies
- Certified Alcohol and Drug Counselor-Certified Addiction Specialist (CADC-CAS)

Robert is one of a handful of men who can be found facilitating, coaching, and supporting fellow inmates within our rehabilitative community almost every night of the week. He has made it his mission to support men in their personal transformation as they pursue unprecedented futures. He mentors at-risk youth through the prison's *We Care Youth Diversion Program* and is committed to sharing the insights and wisdom that others have shared with him. Through his commitment to paying it forward, Robert is living his life as a Man Built for Others.

Chapter 2

*Nobody cares how much you know,
until they know how much you care.*

- Theodore Roosevelt

My transformation began with an awakening, an unearthing of my past, an embracing of my present, and the casting of a vision for my future. I knew that I needed to change my life. My soul was at stake, and I needed to separate myself from the person I had become. I had experienced profound heartache and tragedy that left me in a state of anger, fear, emptiness, and despair. My despair proved to be an emotional environment perfectly suited for my inner villain. It was a dark place where I chose to surrender my God-given greatness.

I was the second son born to young, devoted, and loving parents who immigrated to the United States in the late 1970s and settled in the downtown section of Los Angeles. My mother and father worked extremely hard and gave love to their three children in the same spirit. My mother, a beautiful woman who embodies the strength that only God could bless a mortal with, struggled to raise her three children while attempting to pass on the virtues that she herself possessed. The city of Los Angeles' poverty-stricken ghetto blocks, coupled with the cold-blooded epitaph being authored by its delinquent youth and the booming gang culture, would prove to be a formidable opponent for my mom. With the exception of the prison cells where I have lived for the past 20 years, LA has been the only home I have ever known.

As a kid, I was creative, tender, affectionate, sensitive, and artistic. I spent a lot of time at my brother's side; we were born a year apart, and were inseparable throughout our childhood. My brother and I possessed the same values; however, he displayed them with more integrity. At the same time, he also had a dangerous edge, which I believed that I needed to possess as well. I loved my brother dearly, and I aspired to be like him in our youth. One of the fondest memories I have of our childhood is his willingness to play the villain, which allowed me to be the hero. God gifted him generously with virtues that would have served him as a man, a gift that would never come to full bloom here on Earth.

On a Sunday in May of 1995, my world stopped, and nothing would ever be the same again. On this particular Sunday afternoon, I was sitting in our living room. My brother had just left the house about an hour and a half earlier and went up the street to visit his close friend. Even now, I can remember that day vividly as I heard the bang of five loud blasts ring out suddenly—interrupting the sound of young children playing outside.

The silence that ensued only lasted a moment, but it felt eternal as I intuitively experienced a sickening tightness in my stomach and a suffocating sensation in my heart that filled me with fear. Initially, my mind ran rapid. My thoughts were racing as I arrived at the frightening notion that the five loud blasts came from gunfire and were somehow linked to my brother. As my heart raced and my thoughts pleaded with God for my intuition to have been mistaken, I summoned my legs to run as fast as they were physically able. I ran hard and fast up the hill—a hill that we skateboarded down many times in amusement as kids. On this day, the hill seemed so much steeper. Sprinting up past a car that was bolting in the opposite direction, I took notice in a blur and continued in my race upwards.

Where I grew up, a typical Sunday afternoon was vibrant with joyful children playing innocently with their siblings and neighborhood friends. Families gathered in order to spend time together before the work week began all over again. On this Sunday, however, they would be there to witness the brutal shooting of a young man who they had watched grow up and play on the very same street as their own children—a young man who many considered to be one of their own.

I ran past a small crowd that was gathering until my legs suddenly stopped . . . I had arrived. As I was desperately attempting to catch my breath while I surveyed my destination, I could sense my brother. In fact, I knew it was my brother. Irrationally, I pleaded for it not to be true as I pressed on, advancing towards a neighbor who tugged and pulled on me like a soldier showing concern for a fellow comrade. As I took in the scene, I saw someone pulling him out into the open to offer aid, and my eyes confirmed what my heart had been dreading. My brother's bullet-riddled body was being gently dragged from the dark parking structure where he had attempted to take refuge from the hail of bullets. His body was now being brought in the bright sun light. The last words I remember hearing were, "It's your brother," which escaped from our neighbor's lips as he looked over at me while dragging my brother to the center of the street. I knelt down, pulled my brother close, and cradled his head on my lap. As his blood began covering my palms, I became frantic trying to figure out what I could do as I witnessed my brother's possible last moments. All I could do was speak to him as he gasped for breath through his agony. I could sense his suffering, and the experience tore me up. I yelled at him in anger to hang on, to stay with me, as his will to live appeared to be fading in the midst of his excruciating pain.

My brother had been shot five times, each bullet finding a part of his body to impact. One bullet to the back of the head, one bullet in his back, one bullet in his left leg, and the last two bullets in his right leg. I felt my brother giving in, and I couldn't help him as he endured the agonizing pain. As my brother was dying in my arms, I pleaded with God to not take him. I screamed at my brother to focus on me and to please not go. Cradling him in my arms, I assured him that help was on the way and that everything was going to be okay, even though I did not know if any of that was true. I gently held him while waiting for the paramedics to arrive. A small crowd of people from the neighborhood circled us and watched intently. I was desperate to get my brother the help that he needed as I listened to him wail in anguish—every wail lacerating my heart. I fought to keep my brother alive with all the focus I could muster. Finally, the paramedics arrived and began tending to my brother.

As I was being pulled away by an officer, my only desire was to stay with my brother. Exhausted and numb, I had no energy left to resist as I was escorted a few feet away. My eyes were burning as I blinked through tears. However, I vigilantly kept my eyes fixed on my big brother. Handcuffs were then squeezed tightly around my wrists as an officer pressed my head down below the trunk of his squad car. But none of this mattered. My only concern was for my dying brother. As the paramedics lifted him into the ambulance, my brother let out a loud, bloodcurdling scream that had a crushing effect on me and would haunt me for many years to come.

While my brother laid in an intensive care unit in a coma fighting for his life, I witnessed my mother suffer as her eldest son's fate was out of her hands. In the days that followed, there were many moments in the hospital where I saw sheer terror on my mother's face. The frailty of life had been revealed to my family, and in the process, we had all suffered a grievous wound. The suffering, however, affected my mom in a way that seems uniquely reserved for a mother.

I remember how scared and lost I felt at that time in my life and the anger that followed. I wondered if my brother would pull through and if God was hearing my pleas. I attempted to bargain for my brother's life, realizing in a moment of clarity that I had nothing to offer. Over the course of this experience, I watched my family begin to fall apart. Instead of honoring the values that my mother had instilled in me, I would begin my slow descent into a spirit of malevolence.

Life before the shooting was not all that complex. The gang culture in Los Angeles was violent and deadly; however, my criminality prior to my brother's shooting did not extend beyond vandalism, fist fights, recreational drug use, and loitering. The shooting catapulted me into a new understanding of the street ethos that had claimed so many. I turned my heart towards the darkest of emotions. The impotence and inadequacy I experienced so intensely called for a response, and I intended to respond with venom and violence. I was preparing to become a criminal, and I was going to use vengeance as justification for the choices I was about to make. At the time, I was unwilling to consider the consequences of the choices I was making. I also knew that the virtues that my mother had taught me wouldn't serve me in my depraved state.

After the coma, a hard and long road to recovery, multiple hospital visits, health complications (that would plague my brother throughout the remainder of his life), and a long stint in a physical therapy rehabilitation hospital, my brother had weathered the hardest fight of his young life. My big brother was alive. He wasn't quite the same, but he had survived. For a short time, my mother found some relief. She had an opportunity to recover from the toll that the shooting had taken, but she was completely unaware of the path that I had decided to take.

At the age of sixteen, I began my pursuit of tragedy and disaster. Once on this path, I quickly progressed further into a criminal lifestyle. With every push forward, I was abandoning hope for the future I had dreamt of as a little kid. I had abandoned the values and principles that I had learned at home and pledged myself to an evil belief system. Time would eventually reveal that I was committed to killing myself or another human being by running the streets with other angry and hopeless youths.

As my family tried to recoup a sense of normalcy, I grew cold and indignant towards them—and the world in general. I became hateful, desperate, selfish, deceitful, confused, and violently bitter. I had given up on myself, succumbing to the vile idea of no longer having a choice. I can recall that there were times when I could barely recognize the kid I had been before the shooting. I was dedicated to the friends I grew up with as we became villains who terrorized the city. In my commitment to my criminal lifestyle, I never stopped to consider the pain and suffering that my choices were causing.

On Sunday, September 1, 1996, approximately six weeks into my seventeenth birthday, I committed murder. My criminality escalated to a degree of violence that cost a young man his life and terrorized the lives of others. It was not until a week later, however, while sitting silently in a pair of handcuffs that I would fully realize the tragedy I had caused. I had intentionally passed on the same heartbreaking pain and suffering to the family of my victims that my own family had experienced not so long ago. I had ripped away the hopes that a mother had for her son, and in the process, I had surrendered my humanity.

At the age of eighteen, I was sentenced to 48 years-to-life, and my fall had only begun. I was sent to one of the worst penitentiaries in the state of California, a designated Level 4 maximum-security institution. While there, I would continue my descent into despair as I navigated the dark depths of my evil surroundings. I had committed myself to criminality as I attempted to purge myself of any residual virtue.

There were so many times over the course of my incarceration that I would need to convince myself of my own victimhood in order to justify my criminal behavior. I was unwilling to take responsibility for the harm I had caused so many innocent people. In my villainy, I cast blame at life, at the tragedy of my circumstances, at the kill or be killed ethos of the streets, and all the other destructive thoughts to which I continued giving energy. Thoughts such as, "He would have done the same to me if given the chance," or "He was in the life as much as I was," and "That's just how it goes on the streets." I would use my brother's shooting as evidence to reaffirm how right I was and how screwed up life can be. I was in a shameful and sad state. I was blind, hopeless, and calloused. In my cowardice, I was unwilling to fess up to the suffering I had inflicted, and I continued to blame my victim and his family. Sadly, I spent years running from the truth and responsibility that I would one day need to own.

In late 2001, my brother died. The shooting had numbered his days, and again my mother's heart was broken. Rather than grieve for my brother, I used his death to further justify my criminality. I thought I could run from his death through violence, and after assaulting another inmate, I found myself in Ad-Seg (the Administrative Segregation Housing Unit).

Irrationally, I thought that giving myself over to violence would help me avoid the suffering.

I believed that displaying any sentiment or emotion would be perceived as weakness, and I did my best to remain stoic. I often found myself grieving in silence late at night, hoping that my cellmate wouldn't discover me. I was becoming sick of life. I grew tired of the despair that seemed to accompany me, and again, I decided to run from it all. For the next ten and a half years, I was actively engaged in my criminality. I convinced myself that God had stopped listening for my voice. This was another lie.

In late 2010, I was sent to the Correctional Training Facility (CTF) in Soledad. It was a transfer that I was reluctant to accept, and after arriving, it was a place that I initially despised. My experience of 2010-2011 was filled with darkness. I immediately noticed that I had been transferred to the proverbial end of the line. I thought that this must be where the CDCR sends old prisoners to die. With a 48 years-to-life sentence, I believed that I would most assuredly die at this prison. Each night, as I laid on the cold steel bunk, I considered the possibility that this would be my death bed.

Being confronted with this possible version of my end propelled me to continue immersing myself in destructive behavior. Eventually, I had a fallout with my mother, father, and younger sister over a series of intrusions, disagreements, and old resentments that I kept alive in my heart. Moreover, the woman I had fallen in love with many years ago as a boy (and had remained by my side), grew tired of me in this state. I believe she could no longer bear to witness my self-destruction. My heart was hurting, and I had never been lonelier. Finally, I began thinking that I needed to change my life.

I had run out of earth beneath my feet, and CTF-Soledad was the edge. Nowhere further to go, beaten, and tired, I remembered the wisest advice that my father ever shared with me. He said, "Son, I'm going to fail you, so look to God and ask Him to hold you. And when he does, you hold on as tight as you can." So, on the hard, concrete floor of my prison cell, I bowed on my knees and called out to Jesus with my broken and defeated heart to help me—to restore me what he had planned for my life. Kneeling there, I wept for all of the pain that I had caused so many. In December of 2012, I embarked on a different path, a path of transformation. And the God that I was convinced had grown deaf to my call revealed his love for me as his child. It was here at CTF where I discovered the people whom He had called to do His work within my life. Sometimes, I believe that a good portion of these people were unaware on whose behalf they were actually working, while others knew the calling that God had placed on their lives for serving others. I call many of these men my friends, teachers, mentors, and brothers.

My transformation has been an ongoing process for the past few years and hasn't been without some failures and rebelliousness on my part. However, when I failed, I failed forward; and in my commitment to transformation, I found freedom within these prison walls. What I've come to realize about myself, my life, and this journey, is that God never let go of my hand. He was with me in my youth, He was with me in my suffering, He was with me in my villainy, and He is with me today. In His providence, I have always been accompanied by some beautiful people. These were the individuals who saw past the muck that I was cloaked in and never lost sight of the creative, tender, affectionate, sensitive, and artistic kid that I had been and would be called to be as a willing servant of Jesus Christ.

There are many regrets that I will carry with me. I deeply regret all of the pain and suffering I inflicted on my victim, his mother, his family, and the countless others who I affected through my evil actions and posture of heart. I am committed to walk the endless path of repentance in my transformation.

A pivotal transformational shift occurred in a small classroom with a group of men and one woman, during a three-day workshop. At the end of the second day, I was asked to take the night to cast a ten-year vision for my life with me as the hero of the story. This assignment proved to be a difficult. I was no longer the same little kid who thought of himself as a hero. As I cast my ten-year vision, I allowed myself to think of a future worthy of a man of God, and I haven't looked back since.

Now, several years later, I am still uncomfortable with thinking of myself as a hero. However, I can say with honesty and sobriety that with the strength of my Lord and Savior Jesus Christ, the support of my family and friends, and my commitment to a future worth having, I have secured the personal freedom to do the right thing. I am responsible, and I am present for the people I love. If this is heroic, then I humbly accept that title.

For God, and all the family, friends, and brothers who have given me so much, I love you dearly. Mom, thank you, and I love you.

Men Built for Others Profile

Name: Johnny Howe
Date of Birth: 6/27/72
Sentence: 20 years-to-life
Parole Eligibility: 2017

Leadership Maxim: *There is nothing worse than being unable to tell your own story.*
Person He Is Most Inspired By: Jesus Christ
Favorite Book: The Bible

Education & Interests
- Bachelor of Arts in Behavioral Science
- Certified Alcohol and Drug Counselor-Certified Addiction Specialist (CADC-CAS)

No one has been more active within the self-help community than Johnny. He is known for his passion and kindness for people who are still on the fence—the people who are curious about a new life but are not yet committed to transformation. He is a recruiter of such men and is making a contribution to the growth of the transformational island. He recently married Cynthia, a beautiful woman of God, whom he describes as his best friend and supporter. Today, Johnny lives for Jesus Christ. He strives to be a good husband, and he is dedicated to helping people who are addicted to alcohol, drugs, and the criminal lifestyle. He now lives his life as a Man Built for Others.

Chapter 3

They tried to bury us, but they didn't know we were seeds.

- Dinos Christianopoulos

I was born in Hawthorne, California, and unfortunately raised by the California Youth Authority (CYA) and the California Department of Corrections and Rehabilitation (CDCR). Growing up, I immersed myself in a gang and criminal lifestyle. I sought this lifestyle because I was searching for acceptance, love, and purpose. I do not doubt that my mother loved me, but it was the moments when she wasn't at her best that I used as evidence to convince myself otherwise.

One morning when I was eight years old, I remember walking down the hallway at around 3 AM because I needed to use the bathroom. My mother, who was drunk, called out to me. When I went to her, she told me that the only reason she had me was to keep my dad around. My dad left us before I was even born, and I carried the guilt for that as I grew up. However, I didn't realize the burden until I was almost Forty years old. When I turned fifteen, my mother told me that she knew I was a gang member, that I was selling drugs, and she understood that she couldn't do anything to stop it. When she told me this, part of me was excited because I felt like I was free to do anything I wanted. A bigger part of me, as I later realized, felt abandoned, unloved, and not worth fighting for. This was part of my justification for getting involved in gangs and drugs, which I used to fill these voids in my life.

By the time I was seventeen, I had used these justifications to become an active gang member who would go to any lengths to gain the approval of other criminals. I told myself that receiving praise from the *homies* was the most important thing in the world. I believed that their recognition not only validated me as being a *down homeboy*, but it also provided a distorted sense of belonging which I craved. This twisted way of connecting my self-worth with criminal viciousness eventually resulted in murdering a man during a robbery.

A short time later, I found myself in the Riverside Juvenile Hall wondering what I had gotten myself into. I was told that I was facing the death penalty for robbery and murder, and I'd be tried as an adult. I was afraid. I knew not to show fear and realized the consequences of being seen as "weak" by other inmates. I couldn't risk them taking advantage of me. So that became my mantra, "I will not let anyone punk me, and I will not be a victim."

While I was in juvenile hall, the counselor would allow me to use the phone, and I would call a couple of my homeboys. One of my homeboys told me that my mom had shown up and yelled at them, saying, "He is facing the death penalty, and you don't care." I felt embarrassed, and I was going to let my mom know that day because she was on her way to come visit me. I was sitting there as she walked in and didn't bother getting up when she hugged me. She asked what was wrong. I shared what I heard, and I told her, "I told you not to talk sh*t to my homies." She said, "They don't care about you. They're not going to be there for you." I said, "You don't know my homeboys." She asked me, "Do your homeboys mean more to you than me?" I said, "Yeah." She said, "I come way over here to Riverside from LA to visit you." I said, "Why don't you just leave." She put her head down and started crying, but she didn't leave. We sat there for what seemed like forever, and I felt sad, ashamed, and humiliated for hurting the one woman who I knew in my heart loved me like no other person ever would. We began to talk, and I apologized. This brought us close. And as time passed, I realized that what she said was true, and it was coming from a place of love, protection, and compassion.

As I began to serve my sentence of 20 years-to-life, I quickly learned that those who were unwilling to be violent didn't last long in the California Youth Authority (or YA for short). In order to fit in and be accepted, I made a conscious choice to agree to do anything violent or criminal. I saw how people who tried to prevent violence from happening got treated, and I wanted no part of that. Looking back, I now realize that I lacked the courage to take a stand. In YA, I participated in riots just because it was Friday the 13th or because we had been existing for too long without an incident. I didn't always agree with it, but I went along with it because, once again, I was more concerned with what others thought of me than I was with doing the right thing. I was later asked if I wanted to transfer from that institution (which was located in Northern California), to Y.T.S. (which was in Chino—a southern part of California). Y.T.S. was much bigger and had a lot more to do. There was a gym with weights, a boxing program, a swimming pool, actual dances with girls, and it even had a college program.

One thing that had been weighing on me was the way that my mom looked the first time I saw her after I was arrested for this crime. I had seen her look crushed, disappointed, and hurt in the past, but I had never seen her look so devastated, embarrassed, and let down in my life. I knew I wanted to do something so she could at least hold her head up and be a little proud of her baby boy. She told me that someone told her, "At least my son isn't a murderer." I felt ashamed for when she told me this. I thought back to the one thing that she would always tell me, "No matter what you do, get your education." I figured that maybe I could get involved in the college program. I felt it was a long shot. However, I applied anyway, and to my surprise, I was accepted.

One of the first five classes I had to take was *Introduction to Shakespeare*. I remember having a lot of doubts and fears. I told myself, "I am a gang member. What do I know about Shakespeare?" But I made a decision to do the best that I could, and if college wasn't for me (or if it was too difficult), then I could always go back to being a full-time gang member. I decided to work hard and dedicate myself to my college education the same way I did to my gang and criminal lifestyle. Motivated by the possibility of making my mom proud and removing some of the shame and humiliation I caused her, in a little over two years, I completed all the classes needed to receive my AA degree, and graduated with honors.

Before the ceremony, I told my mom that they were having a screening of a movie that was coming out and that they allowed us to invite our families. When she walked in and recognized that it was a graduation, she was a little surprised. When I was called up to give a speech as the class valedictorian, I watched the smile return to my mother's face, along with a sense of peace and tranquility. These were all of the things that I had stolen the day I called her to tell her that I was charged with murder.

I pulled this same surprise on her when I graduated three years later with my Bachelors of Science in Behavioral Science. Education was a tool that I used to lift my mom's spirits and build my confidence and self-esteem. It helped me believe in myself for the very first time.

Soon after I received my Bachelor's Degree, I was sent to state prison. I was at this new facility for about three months when I was called into the counselor's office. The counselor told me that my mother had passed away. I was devastated. She was the one person I was living for. I was going to college, staying out of trouble, not drinking or using drugs, working on coming home, and now my inspiration was gone. I felt like I had nothing to live for, and to top it off, the governor at the time said "the only way a lifer was going to parole was in a pine box."

Instantly, I became hopeless, and I used this as an excuse to dive headfirst back into a criminal and gang lifestyle. I got involved in numerous illegal activities, but I didn't get caught for anything until 2002 when I was videotaped participating in a riot at Old Folsom. As a result, I was transferred to CTF-Soledad where I continued my criminal behavior and drug addiction.

In 2005, I was denied parole for five years, which was the maximum denial that the Board of Parole Hearings (BPH) could give at that time. After that denial, I continued to live a reckless life and received numerous disciplinary write-ups for possessing cell phones, drugs, drug paraphernalia, and attempting to smuggle a quarter pound of marijuana into the prison. In 2010, after going back in front of the BPH, I was issued a 15-year denial after having already served 20 years.

When I walked out of that hearing, I knew that if I was ever going to get out of prison, I needed to make some changes. The kind of changes that I was thinking about at the time were such things as only getting high on the weekends and using a cell phone every other day instead of every day. I needed to change, and I wanted to change, but I wasn't ready to grow up and be responsible.

There was a guy named Steve who I had known since we were in YA together. I had been in other prisons with him as well, and we eventually ended up in CTF-Soledad together. He was going to self-help programs, and I would ask him why he was going to these things when the governor said the only way we would parole was in a pine box. He responded, "Integrity." I didn't have a clue what that meant, and when I asked him, he said, "Integrity is doing the right thing even when no one was looking."

Steve went to Board after I received the 15-year denial, and was found suitable for parole. A couple of weeks before he was scheduled to go home, he asked me, "If there was someone who was keeping you in prison, and preventing you from going home and being with your family, would you consider that person a friend or an enemy?" I said, "That guy would be my worst enemy." He said, "What are you doing to yourself?" I started to think about that statement, and I realized that all of the trouble I got into, the 15-year denial, and the hopelessness were all a result of the choices I was making. Although this had a profound impact on me, I continued to think that I could get away with some of the things I was doing.

A couple months after this conversation with Steve, I found myself in the hole (Administrative Segregation) for an assault that I wasn't actually involved in. As I sat in the hole, I told myself that this was God's way of getting my attention, and this may be the last chance to get serious about transforming my life. I knew that this transformation had to begin and end with Jesus Christ. I got on my knees and invited him into my life. I asked him to help me stop using drugs, alcohol, and being involved with the criminal lifestyle that I had lived for so many years. The disciplinary write-up for the assault was eventually dismissed, and I was placed back in the general population. After my return, I was offered drugs many times, but I kept the promise that I made with God.

I began going to church and participating in self-help groups. One of the first groups I participated in required us to write out a ten-year vision. I had just been denied 15 years, so I raised my hand and said that I was still going to be in prison. They invited me to dream beyond the prison walls. If I could have any future I wanted, what would it look like? What would I want if I could have anything? So I stayed up until two in the morning writing out my dream for my future. I wanted to use my BA in Behavioral Science to become an alcohol and drug counselor. I wanted a house, a wife, and a motorcycle. I wanted to help coach little league baseball, football, and soccer.

When I returned to the self-help workshop the next day, I was invited to begin living my life from my future vision instead of from my past, which is where I had been making all of my decisions from. Now, my thoughts of always having to be a criminal, drug addict, and gang member were being challenged. I didn't know if these dreams would ever come true, but I had committed myself to hold on to this dream like a kid holds on to a balloon. After I completed that three-day workshop, I would often ask myself if the choice I was about to make was going to bring me closer to my vision or take me away from it. Along with God, this vision became the rudder that I used to guide my ship.

About a year later, I was asked if I would be willing to start taking classes to become an alcohol and drug counselor, and I thought back to how this was part of my dream. I was a little afraid, but I was also very excited because I began to see doors open toward the future that I said I wanted. Once a few of us completed all of the classes that were required to obtain our Alcohol and Drug Specialist I and II certificates, our friend Eugene got released under Proposition 36 (the amendment to the Three Strikes Law). While Eugene was having lunch with an addiction's studies professor to discuss the possibility of helping inmates become certified, there happened to be an Alcohol and Drug Counselor sitting in the adjacent booth. This man overheard their conversation and gave his card to Eugene. Soon thereafter, they began to work on getting what was needed for us to become state certified. With the support of the Crop Organization, we were able to meet the necessary requirements as we prepared ourselves to take the final proctored exam. Eight of us took the test, and we all felt pretty good about how we had performed.

A couple months after we took the test, we were told that everyone passed except for one guy. When I was told that I had passed the test, it felt better than any high from any drug that I had ever taken. I would tell anyone who would listen that I had passed the test. I was finally going to be more than just an alcoholic, drug addict, criminal, and gang member. This gave me a type of confidence and self-assurance that I had never known before. When Eugene went to pick up the actual certifications, he learned that there had been a mix-up and I was the one who had failed the test.

I had just gotten off the phone after having a very disturbing conversation, and I was sitting on the bleachers when a friend of mine who was involved with the ADS program approached me. He looked concerned and said that he had to talk to me about something. He said, "You know how we said that you passed the certification test? Well, there was a mistake, and you were actually the one who didn't pass the test." My heart dropped, and I sat there in disbelief as the yard was being recalled. It felt like I had actually been punched in the stomach. I was devastated. I sat there with my head down feeling like a complete failure. I told myself, "See, you will never be anything more than a criminal, a gang member, and an addict. What were you thinking? Stay in your lane and stop embarrassing yourself. Now everyone will know what a failure you are."

I went back to my cell feeling worthless, hopeless, and deflated. An older Christian gentleman came up to me and said, "When you go in the cell, thank God for all that you do have." It wasn't easy, but I got on my knees, thanked God for what I did have, and I asked for strength and courage to get through it. I was reminded of Philippians 1:6, which says, "And I am certain that God, who began the good work within you, will continue his work until it is finally finished on the day when Christ Jesus returns."

I was told that I could retake the test, but I was afraid of failing it again. I remembered how humiliated I felt when I found out that I failed the first time, and I never wanted to experience that again. I thought about my vision, and the conversation I had with Steve about being my own worst enemy, and I asked myself if I was going to continue to live like a coward. The decision I was about to make would determine if I would let go of the dream I had been working toward just because things were not going the way I had planned towards.

I began to study for the test again and felt overwhelmed with the thought of how I would look if I failed. When I finally walked into the classroom to retake the test, I was less sure about passing it than I was during the first exam. I prayed for God's will to be done and trusted that He had my best interest in mind. When I would think about failing the test, I would remind myself that my life couldn't go forward if I was focused on the past. Whenever I heard that negative voice tell me I was a failure and that I would never amount to anything, I would repeat Philippians 4:13, "I can do all things through Christ who strengthens me."

I was sitting in church, and I knew that the results of my exam were coming in soon. I was thinking to myself that if I really wanted to help someone, I didn't need a piece of paper to do that. The Pastor said, "In order for someone to be happy, something needs to happen, but we can all experience joy because joy comes from the Lord." Later that week, a friend involved in the ADS program told me that I passed the exam.

Not long afterwards, I filed documents to appear back in front of the Parole Board to be considered for parole. As a result of participating in (and facilitating) several self-help groups, becoming certified as an Alcohol and Drug Counselor, and staying out of trouble, I received a response two weeks later stating that I was scheduled for a hearing that would take place in five months. I was grateful for an opportunity to be back in front of the Board ten years early. I felt really good about the possibility of being paroled because I hadn't been in trouble for six years, and I had done everything that was asked of me. Even though I had some expectations to be found suitable for parole, I would have said that I trusted in God and believed that whatever happened in the Board Room would be God's will. When I walked out of the hearing with a three-year denial, however, the look on my face said that I didn't trust in anyone but myself. I even questioned God's plan and realized that I had very little faith.

As I laid there in bed tossing and turning all night, I was disappointed, embarrassed, and ashamed. I felt like I had let a lot of people down. I was feeling sorry for myself, and I began throwing a pity party, but no one showed up. I got up at 4:15 AM and began my daily prayer and meditation. As I was listening to God, I was reminded that I got exactly what I asked for, His will. The denial just meant a delay. I asked God for strength and understanding to help me through it. I read a passage that morning in the Daily Bread that said having a good attitude is like putting windshield wipers on your car. They don't prevent it from raining, but they help us see more clearly so we can get to where we want to go. When I walked out of the cell that morning, a friend of mine named Raymond came up to me and said, "I believe God kept you here so that you could keep helping me." I believe this was God using Raymond to remind me that it was not yet my time to go home. I realized that I had more work to do with my own walk, as well as in supporting others with their personal transformations.

I am not yet the man that I will someday become, but I am no longer the criminal, addict, and gang member that I once was. I am committed to serving Jesus Christ and continuing to trust in God's plan for my life. I am committed to living a life that inspires others who are addicted to alcohol, drugs, gangs, and a criminal lifestyle to pursue a future worth having. I am also committed to providing love, support, and direction to those who need it, want it, and have the courage to choose something new for their lives.

Men Built for Others Profile

Name: James Arthur Willock
Date of Birth: 12/08/72
Sentence: 34 years-to-life
Parole Eligibility: 2020

Leadership Maxim: *Life is about moments and relationships; each moment is an opportunity to build relationships.*
Person He Is Most Inspired By: Anne Frank and Nelson Mandela
Favorite Book: *Diary of a Young Girl* by Anne Frank

Education & Interests
- GED
- Poet

James is serious about serving people. He sees it as his duty and is diligent about preparing himself to help others. He is a natural lifter and encourager. He believes that people want to change their lives and that they need to know that people care. Well, James cares. He is willing to perform the humblest of duties and says that "*no task is too small.*" Recently, he assembled *Team Heart* and raised $1,000 for CTF's Relay-4-Life fundraiser to help in the fight against cancer. Whether in prison or the free world, James is committed to being a good man, and through honoring this commitment, he is living his life as a Man Built for Others.

Chapter 4

Great occasions do not make heroes or cowards; they simply unveil them to the eyes of men. Silently and imperceptibly, as we wake or sleep, we grow strong or weak; and at last some crisis shows what we have become.

- Brooke Foss Westcott

My first life-changing experience happened when I was eight-years-old. I didn't have the greatest childhood. For as long as I could remember, I had lived with my mother and her abusive boyfriends (or with her and some of my other dysfunctional family members). But when I turned eight, for the first time in my short life, my mother, sister, and I moved into our first apartment. In fact, this was the only time that we (just the three of us) lived together as a family. Things began to change, however, when my biological father got out of prison and came to live with us. Before this, the only real memory I had of him was going to Jamestown State Prison a few months prior to his release for a family visit.

My sister's biological father, Al, remained in our lives and continued to show me love and attention. I even went with my sister on several weekends to visit him at his house. Looking back, he was the only adult male that I remember being in my mother's life who didn't abuse her and wasn't into criminal activity. I felt love and respect for him, but deep down, I longed for my biological father.

I remember the day that my dad got out of prison. I stayed up late into the night waiting for him until my mother eventually made me go to bed. I still tried to stay awake until he arrived, but I fell asleep with my clothes on. I awoke with my mother yelling for me to go let my father inside. I jumped up and flew down the stairs. I can still remember the sound of the coins that I had saved to buy my dad a present falling out of my pocket and hitting the stairs as I ran. When I opened the door for him, I was the happiest kid alive.

About a week after his return, and with my father's urging, I went for a weekend visit with my sister to Al's house. When we came back, there was a different mood in the apartment. I didn't know it at the time, but my mom and dad were doing drugs.

Shortly after this, my father took me to the store and taught me how to steal. We stole fake guns that looked real so he could rob people for money to buy drugs. I was scared, but because I desperately wanted to make my father proud, I did whatever he told me to do. A few crimes later, things got even worse. One night, I awoke to the sounds of my mother crying and my father loudly telling her to be quiet. I ran to their room, opened the door, and found my father pinning my mother to the bed with his knees and hands. Her face was bloody, and I yelled for him to get off of her. He ordered me to get out, saying that it was none of my business, and he demanded that my mom tell me the same thing.

I was crying and confused. I wanted to protect my mother, and I wanted to please my father so that he would stay. My mom told me to call my grandfather so he could come and get my dad. I didn't know his number, so I ran down the stairs and dialed zero. I was in the third grade, and that's what I was taught to do for help. Through my sobs, I told the operator that I needed my grandfather's number. The operator asked, "Why?" and I told her, "So he can come get my father who is beating my mother." You can probably guess what happened next. The police came and arrested my father. I remember him being mad at me as he was being taken to the police cruiser in handcuffs. To my surprise, both my mother and my grandparents were mad at me for calling the operator and the resulting arrest of my father.

While growing up, I created a story about these events that shaped and reinforced my criminal beliefs and actions. I then sought out friendships with those who thought and acted like me. From a very young age, I decided to be a distrustful and bitter criminal. I have broken into people's homes, I have sold drugs, I have robbed people, and I have let other people take the fall for my crimes. I was a gangbanging criminal who blamed my parents and my environment for the choices I made.

This turmoil resulted in me spending my early teen years moving from one place to another. I usually lived with relatives and friends, but I was eventually made a ward of the state by social services where I went from group home to group home. My mother was sent to prison for attempted murder after getting into a fight and stabbing a woman. This allowed me to justify the bitterness that I felt about my situation, and I felt victimized as I thought that everyone was against me.

When I was nineteen, I murdered a man. After committing this terrible act, I knew that I was in desperate need of transformation. Facing a life sentence for murder, I immediately gave up gangbanging. The sad part is that I knew when I was on the streets that the gang lifestyle (and all of its promises) were a lie, so that was actually pretty easy for me to leave behind. I wasn't as willing, however, to give up on my belief that the system was unjust and racist. In my mind, this belief justified my bitterness, anger, and victimized attitude.

After giving up my allegiance to the gang, I turned to God. But, I still had a victim's perspective and a criminal mindset. Before going to prison, I met some Nation of Islam members who introduced me to the Final Call (The Nation's Newspaper) and their teachings. So while I was in the county jail awaiting trial for murder (and looking for someone to blame for my life and my crimes), I turned to the Nation of Islam's interpretation of God, the Bible, and the Quran. According to this perspective, the White man and the system were really to blame for crime. Everything I read from the Nation fit right into my irresponsible beliefs and way of being. I could be a "man of God" and still blame other people and external circumstances for my actions and my attitude. Even though I robbed people, lied to people, shot people, sold drugs, and murdered a man, I could still see myself as a good guy. At the conclusion of my trial, I was convicted of first-degree murder with the use of a firearm. When I was sentenced to 34 years-to-life for the murder and a prior juvenile gang enhancement, I called the judge a racist. I then blamed him, the system, and my victim for everything that was happening to me.

When I entered the prison system, I brought those beliefs and my criminal worldview with me. I found others who shared my outlook, and even though we called ourselves "men of God," we functioned and thought like a gang. It was the same mentality that we professed to be against, but we only associated with other Blacks that shared our criminal worldview. We didn't practice charity, forgiveness, or understanding; instead, we did the opposite.

I've now been in prison for twenty-five, and for about the first twenty years, this was who I was committed to being. I've had 16 Rules Violation Reports (write-ups) ranging from disrespecting staff, possessing cell phones, perpetrating violence, and possessing inmate manufactured weapons. I have also received five less serious write-ups called 128s (information that staff thought needed to be noted in my file), and I've been placed in disciplinary isolation units three times. I made a lot of superficial changes over my first twenty years of incarceration, but I maintained the same belief system. Even when I wasn't actively engaged in serious or violent crime, I continued to think and behave criminally. I used my beliefs about the system being corrupt, racist, and oppressive to justify why it was okay for me to break the rules.

The more I read and the more I interacted with different people over the years, the more I learned. Through reading the Quran (and not books of people's opinions about the Quran), I eventually discovered that the White man was not "the devil" and that a racist is a racist regardless of skin color. I stopped believing the Nation's teachings a long time ago. I have since realized that not all Muslims are good and America isn't against me or anyone else just because they are Black or Muslim.

A pivotal moment in my transformation came in 2012 while working with an older White man named Harvey Hawks. A few of my fellow co-workers (two Blacks and one Hispanic) told me that he was a racist. Harvey and I worked in a confined space and spent a lot of time together, and over time, we got to know each other. I discovered that he wasn't racist, but rather, he was a hard worker who didn't like lazy people or those who were still into criminal behavior. I also found out that my other co-workers were all of the things that Harvey didn't like. We haven't had any contact since he was paroled (after having served over twenty years or so in prison), but Harvey touched my life in a way that he never knew.

One weekend, on the Monday before he was going home, Harvey and I were organizing a sport's tournament together.

Harvey said to me, "Ansar, I'll be gone when the coach comes back, so make sure my chrono gets into my work file." I was stunned. He was going home in two days. So I said, "Why the hell do you care about a chrono." He said, "Ansar, you are who you are all of the time, and I'm a programmer for the rest of my life." (A programmer is prison lingo meaning a responsible person.) I know those may not sound like words of wisdom spoken by Gandhi or Martin Luther King, but for a man like myself who said (and believed) that I was committed to going home, that statement was profound.

I started to ask myself, "Who am I? What am I committed to? What do I believe?" As I started going to self-help groups, I became willing to put myself on the line in front of other men who had different ethnic backgrounds, believed in different religions, and belonged to different age groups. I completely opened myself up to the process and allowed myself to be vulnerable. I started getting to know other men who I had been living around for the previous 20 or so years. I started seeing them with new eyes, and this new way of relating to people even affected the way I saw the prison staff. I began to see everyone as their own unique person. I now have friends, not comrades, homies, or dawgs.

In the past, I looked for other people and circumstances to blame for my crimes and actions. I blamed others, because like many other human beings, I was afraid. I was afraid to take responsibility—afraid to see myself as weak, wrong, or bad. Yet, it was only through taking responsibility that I have found the power to transform myself and the situations in my life. Playing the victim helped me get to where I am today—a forty-four-year-old man who has spent 25 years in prison for the murder of another human being. Now, it's time for something brand new, and for me, that means RESPONSIBILITY.

When I started to take responsibility for the results that I have in my life—which includes my crimes, my incarceration, and my attitude—everything shifted in a more productive and positive direction. In the years since my talk with Harvey, I got rid of my illegal cell phone and stopped engaging in other criminal activity entirely. I went from someone who believed it was impossible to avoid getting into trouble in prison, to someone who is dedicated to helping others see that they can choose to live responsibly no matter where they are. By taking responsibility for my life, both the good and the bad, I have discovered the power to be present in my relationships and transform my attitude in loving ways from moment to moment. The bitterness and the blame are finally gone, and I am becoming the man that God created me to be.

Men Built for Others Profile

Name: Richard Nunez
Date of Birth: 8/28/66
Sentence: 25 years-to-life
Parole Eligibility: 2023

Leadership Maxim: *Live life with intentionality, for success is paved with it.*
Person He Is Most Inspired By: His mother, J. R. Nunez
Favorite Book: The Bible

Education & Interests
- Associate of Arts in Behavioral Science
- Certified Alcohol and Drug Counselor-Certified Addiction Specialist (CADC-CAS)

For Richard, being of service is a priority. He has assumed responsibility for serving the Spanish-speaking population, and he has accepted several leadership roles within the broader community. Through his service, he has found meaning, purpose, and freedom, and he believes that being a servant is his duty. He is committed to becoming more intimate with God and growing into the man that God created him to be. As a result of his transformation, he has become an authentic leader and is living his life as a Man Built for Others.

Chapter 5

Treat others as you would want to be treated.

The Golden Rule

I was born into a family of six sisters and three brothers. My siblings and I were raised in a poor suburban part of Guadalajara, Mexico, in a two-bedroom house that was rather modest and situated right across from the town's cemetery. That in itself was creepy—but not necessarily a serious problem. What was of true concern was the systemic poverty, lack of parental supervision, scarcity of role models, limited opportunities for progress, abundance of mischief, government corruption, scarcity of schools, and other challenges in the environment. These were the conditions that were present early in my life, and they placed me at an early disadvantage. Although my parents had no education, were of low means, and possessed no professional skills, their love and desire for us to prosper was on par with the most successful and brightest parents.

In spite of their shortcomings, they identified that our living environment was dangerous and impoverished. This observation played an influential role in them deciding to migrate to the United States. Unfortunately, by the time my parents made their decision, the seed of wickedness had been sown by the poor choices I was making at an early age. I didn't know it at the time, but a year later, this seed would bear fruit in a horrific manner.

When I was seven-years-old, I had my first experience with an intoxicating substance (glue). This experience was soon followed by other reckless behaviors such as playing with matches (and lighting the house curtains on fire), stealing money out of the cash register from my parents' small business, venturing away from home without permission, gambling with other kids, harassing the town's prostitutes, and getting into physical altercations. During these early years of delinquency, I also witnessed the accidental drowning of my little sister, which had a traumatic effect on how I viewed life.

Unconsciously, I brushed most of this off as a rite of passage that almost every kid goes through. In hindsight, however, I realize that I was the epitome of an at-risk youth who was heading toward disaster. Apparently, my parents noticed that I was going astray and decided to migrate to the United States. Upon our arrival to our new country, I was thrilled by the abundance of resources, the beauty, the vast number of opportunities available, the kindness of many citizens, and the diversity of people. At the same time, I was overwhelmed, saddened, and intimidated by the socioeconomic disparities, the different language, the new culture, the racism, and apparent inequality. Initially, I struggled to adjust, but I eventually began to appreciate the new culture, the differences, and the vast richness of this country.

From the time of our arrival until the age of nineteen, the notion of "The American Dream" was as true to me as the air I was breathing. I went to prom, proudly graduated from high school, owned my first car, visited Disneyland and other theme parks, held a decent job, was invited to visit the White House, met a state senator at the nation's capital, had several great friends, and fell in love. I was truly living "The American Dream."

Sadly, not long after my high school graduation, I experienced my first real obstacle to achieving my dreams. I discovered that my immigration status precluded me from pursuing a university education. Learning this was a hard blow. I became depressed, disgruntled, and felt betrayed by the country that I had come to love. Unable to continue with a college education, I landed a menial job at a movie theater. It was there that my nefarious childhood behavior made a nasty resurgence.

One day, a co-worker invited me to drink some beers after work. Not wanting to be perceived as unfriendly, I indulged. The events that followed this decision would forever change my life. It was on this particular evening that I was introduced to the drug crack cocaine. I was unaware at the time, but from the moment I first said, "Yes, I'll try it," I was caressing the face of evil. The desire to blame my co-worker for my demise is tempting, and for some people, it might help them to sleep more easily. But as I look at the situation through the rearview mirror, I accept that what transpired on that day was of my own making. I could easily have said no, but instead, I chose to say yes. How come? The truth is that I wanted this to happen. As I referenced earlier, I was struggling with the disappointment of not being able to go to college, and cocaine seemed like an easy way to feel good about myself. Of course, I now see this thinking for the lie it was, but back then, I chose the lie in order to escape my responsibility. I abandoned reason and logic for nothing more than carnal satisfaction. The events that progressed from my decision to smoke crack cocaine were nothing short of nightmarish, and they continue to take a toll thirty years later. The 25 years-to-life prison sentence I am currently serving is a testament to the destructive nature of a lifestyle driven by the use crack cocaine.

So far, I've given a synopsis of my early delinquency without any specific examples of my outright criminal behavior. The truth of the matter is that I feel ashamed that there's so much fabric to cut from. As I previously mentioned, the first time I smoked crack cocaine was with a co-worker. The second time was when a complete stranger approached me and asked me if I wanted to buy what he called "big ones" (meaning big rocks). Outwardly, I shrugged off his offer, but the temptation was intoxicating. After giving into to this strong desire, I realized there was no co-worker to blame. I had become the victim of my own indulgence. It became apparent that a selfishly destructive spirit dwelled within me, and I was willing to do anything to gratify it.

I did not care about consequences. Distinctions between right and wrong became irrelevant as I mutated into a visceral creature. My first and subsequent experiences of smoking cocaine produced a euphoric and relieving sensation that served to reinforce my idolizing perception of the drug. Feeling good became more important than doing right, and I was willing to ignore the danger as long as I could feel that rush.

This attitude resulted in me turning defiant and dangerous. I was lawless, took perilous risks, disrespected others, became an introvert, abandoned any sense of responsibility, and harmed countless people as I distanced myself from God. In addition, using crack cocaine is an extremely expensive habit to maintain. A heavy crack smoker can easily spend $1,000 to $3,000 a day. Multiply that by 365 days a year, and it quickly becomes apparent that a crack habit is financially unsustainable for most people. Furthermore, my lifestyle included other expenses like purchasing liquor and cigarettes for both me and my friends and regularly soliciting prostitutes—the sum of which became almost astronomical. Where does a minimum wage earner get all this money to support such a monster habit? It was certainly not from any lawful avenues. At first, I would support my habits through my paycheck. But in due time, the addiction became ferocious, and my wages proved inadequate to keep up with my indulgences. This was a major factor that sent my life into a tailspin.

The first sign that my criminality was progressing came when I began to pawn my possessions, and unbeknownst to my family, their valuables as well. Initially, I would go back and pay the loan to retrieve them, but that didn't last long. As my habit grew, I was no longer able to repay the loans, and I lost the items I pawned. Many of these valuables held sentimental value for my family, which left them devastated after finding out what I had done. Some of my family members still hold a grudge towards me for betraying their trust.

Eventually, pawning valuables progressed to outright stealing. On one occasion, I remember going to my parent's house when they were at work and stealing the microwave so I could purchase more crack. As I was leaving, I even took a couple of garbage bags full of recyclable aluminum cans for gas money. Breaking my family's heart had become almost normal for me, and they came to realize how serious my problem had become. My craving for crack had become so strong that everyone, including my family, was fair game. After several disgraceful acts of thievery, my family was no longer willing to trust me. I violated the most sacred household principle—I violated my family's peace of mind and security.

To alleviate the criticism and shame, I left home and adopted a new family—a crew of crooks, thieves, prostitutes, liars, cheaters, traffickers, gang members, and junkies. While in their company, not only did I indulge in excessive cocaine consumption, but I participated in numerous criminal acts such as home and auto burglaries, armed robberies, drug trafficking, extortion, and schemes of exploitation. I was willing to do anything that facilitated the acquisition of more drugs.

Another aspect of my lifestyle was that I would solicit the services of prostitutes and disregard the inevitable consequences of unprotected sex. To my good fortune, I didn't get infected with AIDS, but I did catch other sexually transmitted diseases (STDs). That fact by itself is frightening. But what is even more horrific was that when I became aware that I was infected with an STD, I would continue to carelessly engage in sexual relationships with women; thus, putting their health in jeopardy as well.

These are embarrassing and shameful episodes of my life; however, the worst harm that I've caused occurred during the several armed robberies that I committed. Shoplifting and burglaries were bad enough, but when I decided to start robbing people at gun point, I took my criminality to a whole new level of wickedness. I still remember the terrible fear on my victims' faces. The pain and suffering that I made them go through far exceeds most of my other criminal acts. When I aimed my gun at people's faces, they became paralyzed, confused, powerless, and terrified.

I chose to harden my heart and shut my ears to my victims' pleas. What mattered to me was getting money for the next fix, regardless of who suffered in the process. Once I decided to carry out an act, I would develop tunnel vision and become fixated. I came to despise reason, I chose not to care, I was a habitual liar, I became manipulative, and I was loveless. During my criminal career, I not only caused havoc, pain, suffering, and loss of property, but I also ruined the dreams and goals of my family, friends, and others.

In addition to harming innocent people, I've also inflicted physical harm to myself. I would go on drug binges for three to six months at a time while going weeks with practically no sleep and a minimal amount of eating. Taking care of my health was not a priority. Spending money on food meant that I would have less money for drugs, so I chose crack as my sustenance. I would often be so hungry that I would eat out of dumpsters. I became so tired from sleep deprivation that I would sleep on the streets or vacant premises. I went through life with an attitude of careless despair. I now understand my mistake in not thinking about the future. The sleepless nights and periods of starvation have taken a serious toll on my body, and the fact is that my days are numbered.

Perhaps the most important area in my life where I continue to reap the negative consequences of my criminality is in my relationships. The fact that there are less than a handful of people from my past who even care to communicate with me serves as a testimony to the damage that I've caused in people's lives. This realization brings great sadness to my heart, but it also serves as a reminder that many people continue to suffer from my actions.

Making amends to those that I've harmed is an essential first step, and there's much amending to do. From the shameful objectification of victims whom I had never met, to violent encounters with people I claimed to love, my desire to live as an irresponsible criminal damaged countless lives and relationships.

Some people have the belief that when criminals are sent to prison, they cease to transgress. In my case, the opposite was true. Once in prison, I refined my criminality and proceeded with the march of inflicting misery on my fellow prisoners. While in confinement, I disguised my nefarious behavior under the umbrella of "it's all about business." This attitude permitted me to justify the sale and consumption of narcotics while I contributed to the poisoning of minds and added to the financial and emotional burdens of innocent families.

As I share my story, it's obvious that I have harmed the lives of many people, including my own. What is difficult to fathom is why I chose to allow this state of mind to prevail for so long. My road to this recognition has been painful. However, after many years of struggle and self-deception, God's mercy and enlightenment have shined upon me. It was during my sixth year of a 25 years-to-life sentence when I decided to enroll in a community college that offered correspondence courses. My old dream of going to college had resurrected in the most unimaginable place. Not knowing what to expect, and not having much faith in myself, I only enrolled in two courses. To my surprise, by the end of the semester, I had completed both courses with an "A." It was an awesome feeling, but because I was still skeptical, I only enrolled in two more courses the following semester. Once again, I received two "A"s for my work, which boosted my self-esteem.

Three years later, I successfully obtained an Associate's Degree and a Business Certificate with a 4.0 GPA. Unlike my previous experiences where defeat ruled, reaching these achievements was a positive life changer. I felt like I had finally accomplished something meaningful. Surely, this was something to be proud of.

Although I had made great strides academically, I still felt like something was missing internally, which created a void inside of me. This void prompted me to continue looking for answers about why drugs had played such a destructive role in my life and why it was so difficult for me to quit. This spirit of curiosity inspired me to further my education, and I enrolled in a second college that offered alcohol and drug studies (ADS) classes. With hard work and dedication, I finally answered many of the questions that tormented me for decades.

The next step towards my recovery occurred when Ted Gray and Richard Mireles invited me to attend a 3-day seminar. What transpired during this seminar was healing, transformational, and inspiring. Not only did this seminar help me see the light at the end of the tunnel, but it gave me a voracious appetite for self-help programs. Half a year after finishing the ADS courses, I took the necessary steps to become a state certified alcohol and other drug (AOD) counselor.

Crossing paths with Ted Gray, Richard Mireles, and Jesse Bonderman was monumental. Through their commitment, time, and transformational coaching skills, they encouraged me to abandon my maladaptive thinking and malevolent behavior. The most valuable lesson that I learned during this time was that my worst enemy was not some external entity. Rather, it was my way of thinking and behaving that led me to self-sabotage and self-deceive most of my life. At the same time, they also taught me that an infinite world of possibilities and capabilities resides within me. I began to believe that my circumstances do not have to define me—in spite of adversity, I have choices that can either help me transcend or keep me in a cycle of self-pity, anger, hate, and blame. Spending time with these men taught me that meaningful relationships are the true essence of life.

It must be said that my rehabilitation, academic achievements, and improvements didn't occur by osmosis or overnight. It required a lot of work, time, discipline, effort, commitment, intention, and many long nights of studying. Sobriety and rehabilitation doesn't just happen, one must want it and intentionally pursue the results they want in life.

My experience of prison has been filled with years of monotony, loneliness, stress, hostility, lamentation, and sadness. The affliction I have suffered was the result of my stubbornness, lawlessness, and poor choices. I'm the definition of a self-inflicted wound. Having spent twenty years of my life incarcerated, I've missed countless family events; for example, numerous birthdays, graduations, Christmases, death's of loved ones, and times when they became ill. Sadly, my loved ones have also been punished by my incarceration.

I came into prison as a young and vibrant man. Most of that has withered away. Certainly, my vitality is not the same as when I was first convicted. However, not all has been bad. As I've grown older, great strides have been made in other areas of my life. Maturity, along with intentionality, has facilitated the process for me to become more responsible, wise, patient, sociable, and caring.

College helped me to value myself, to elevate my self-efficacy, to treasure knowledge, to consider other possibilities, and to search for life's meaning. Once this occurred, a whole new world came into existence. The third, and most important transformational moment occurred when I made peace with God, which permitted me to establish a personal relationship with Him. Once I did this, I stopped utilizing my energies to war against God. Today, I use my energy to build bridges of understanding, obedience, reverence, and love. Through reconciliation with God, my heart was softened and my posture of rebellion, destruction, stupidity, selfishness, and hate began to disappear. The veil of wickedness that had me blind came off the moment I accepted God into my heart. Most importantly, reconciling with God influenced me to reflect on the purpose of my stay in this world. I've wasted many years representing the banner of evil, and I am now certain that God has other intentions for my life.

The choices I made early in life have slapped me hard, but today I'm making new choices that show great favor and mercy. The future that I envision is one where I take advantage of life in an assertive manner while staying mindful that I live in a diverse society where other people's concerns matter as much as my own. I've come to realize that my purpose in life is not about me—it is about something greater than me. What were we made for? I don't have an answer for you, but for me, the answer came from the critical step of establishing spiritual communication with God.

Thirty years ago when I succumbed to the deceptive story that I told myself about crack cocaine, I set in motion a destructive chain reaction that harmed many. I believe that this was a deviation from my designed purpose. Veering off track has been a waste of time, loss of opportunities, squandering of talent, and depletion of resources. My greatest tragedy are not my fumbles, shortcomings, or feebleness, but that I was unwilling to see that I am truly capable of achieving things beyond my imagination. I realize that the strength that prevails in me today is stronger than the negativity of my past.

Although learning my lesson came at a huge price, I am one of the fortunate ones. Some take their wisdom, capabilities, and un-repentance to their graves. I'm choosing not to take this route. The phenomenal adversities that I've faced and overcome have enabled me to accumulate a treasure trove of life experiences. My intention is to share my experiences with those who are living a criminal life, who are drug addicts, who are on a path of self-destruction, or anyone else who will gain value from hearing my testimony. Like an architect, I'm now in the business of building. Giving back is my new mantra. Surely, I could never fully atone for all my wrongdoings. Nevertheless, I will spend the rest of my natural years bringing healing by sharing my life story and by being of service. I will focus on how I can help instead of what I can take.

The truth is that I'm tired of being my own worst enemy. There's nothing to be proud of when one belittles him or herself. However, that's exactly what I've done most of my life. I mastered the craft of depreciating myself. Fortunately, I've shifted away from that. My new driving force in my affairs is the motto that gave credence to the Cesar Chavez movement—"Si se puede" (Yes I/we can). There is no doubt in my mind that I'm more than the sum of my past results.

I want to be an obedient Christ follower; a good son, brother, uncle, and friend; a caring neighbor; and an influential citizen. I'm aware that *having* the knowledge, skills, comprehension, and capabilities about what it means to be a good person are certainly important. Likewise, knowing what to *do* in order to be accepted as a good person is equally essential. However, what's more ambitious and desirable is not only (having or doing) but *being* the essence of good. If I can *be* those characteristics that I mentioned above, not only will I give the devil a black eye, but I might somehow atone for the harm that I've inflicted on humanity.

Men Built for Others Profile

Name: Manuel Dunn
Date of Birth: 10/22/77
Sentence: 16 years-to-life
Parole Eligibility: 2017

Leadership Maxim: *Everything in life worth living for is worth fighting for.*
Person He Is Most Inspired By: His mother
Favorite Book: The Bible

Education & Interests
- Associate of Arts in Behavioral Science (in progress)
- Certified Alcohol and Drug Counselor-Certified Addiction Specialist (CADC-CAS)

Manuel is known for his honesty and standing like a rock in his commitment to separate himself from the gang culture and lifestyle. He willingly shares his testimony, and provides gang members with an example of transformation. Today, Manuel honors his parents, loves his wife and children, and is extremely proud of his oldest son who serves his country in the United States Marine Corp. Transformations like Manuel's are rare. He has no titles, but he lives his life as an example for others, supports men in their transformation, and lives his life as a Man Built for Others.

Chapter 6

Some of the greatest battles will be fought within the silent chambers of your own soul.

- Ezra Taft Benson

I was thirty-four-years-old when I finally came to realize that every meaningful battle that I had ever fought was internal. This was also the year that my life began to actually feel meaningful, as it was also the year that I found a purpose for my life.

I was born on October 12, 1977, and as I write my story, I am only a few weeks into my 39th year. I feel privileged to turn thirty-nine, because during my adolescent years, the chances of me reaching my 18th birthday were slim at best. Due to the gang wars in Los Angeles, most of the young men who shared my lifestyle felt the same way. The truth is that no one in my neighborhood thought they would make it out of the city. Most of us thought that the only way out would be in a casket or going to prison. I witnessed many childhood friends die in the mean streets of LA, and it saddens me to think about all of the friends I've lost. I am also angered and ashamed to know that I became one of those who so callously disregarded the life of another human being.

I was born in Ecuador. However, at the tender age of four, my parents made the decision to leave their native land in hopes of giving their children a better and brighter future. Not knowing what to expect, Pedro Dunn (my father) and Maria Yolanda Dunn (my mother) brought the eight of us to Los Angeles, California—the place known as the land of milk and honey. Our first residence was 29th Street and Vermont, a well-known and gang-infested area. It was the city I called home for the next several years of my life. In 1988, we moved from 29th Street and Vermont, and my dad made it clear that he wanted to live next to his brother (my uncle Didimo). So our family moved to what we kids called "The Hill" on Berendo Street.

It was on "The Hill" that I began to find the gang culture intriguing. Three of my cousins were well-known *Drifters* gang members. Now that we lived in the same apartment complex, I was able to hang out with them frequently. My cousin, Juan, who was older and had the most influence and respect, was a father figure to most of the neighborhood kids. While I did have a father and two older brothers, I hardly ever spent time with them. Juan never had a problem with any of us hanging around him; in fact, he seemed to enjoy it.

As the years passed, I started to notice how my cousin gained his status in his gang. He was a very violent person, and he never backed down from anyone. He would resolve his problems with violence, and many people feared him because of this. I later realized that it was fear, and not respect, that was displayed by many members of his gang. It did not matter to me how he got it—all that mattered at that time was that I wanted it.

I was the kid who was always picked on while growing up. I was teased and called names because of my hand-me-down clothes and Payless shoes. I was called Indio, and stinky because of my bowl haircut and poor hygiene. I began to develop low self-esteem and feelings of insecurity, and I felt unworthy of love. For those reasons, my cousin's lifestyle seemed extremely enticing. He had respect, money, and fame. I became attracted to these things and to the way people looked at him, admired him, and praised him. People wanted to be around him, but most importantly, they showed him deference. I wanted what he had. From 1988 to 1992, I developed criminal tendencies. My criminal behavior began with things like stealing and fighting. However, that was only the beginning, and eventually, my criminality progressed into more destructive behaviors.

After the 1992 Los Angeles' riots, my parents once again made the decision to move. Part of the reason was to get me away from the gang lifestyle. What made their decision final was the near-death experience I had when a childhood friend got shot by a gang member who was attempting to steal my bike. That event scared my mother. So my father decided to move us, and just like that, we were on the road again.

We settled in the city of Bell Gardens. Unfortunately, things did not get any better. By then, I had become protective of the image that I developed while living in Los Angeles. I was not a gang member yet, but I had already picked up their criminal traits.

New friendships meant new problems. Now at the age of fourteen, my friends Steven and Alex introduced me to a new lifestyle. We began to engage in what was then known as "clubbing." This is where I picked up my dance skills, something that was best kept secret while involved with gangs. However, things were not always peaches-and-cream. Moving into a new environment (with new personalities and lots of attitude) only meant more trouble. Most of the time, we got into jams over girls or because I was a newcomer who was unfamiliar to the local kids. Needless to say, I made more enemies than friends while living in Bell Gardens. I was constantly fighting. I would never turn down a fight because my cousin and father taught me that turning down a fight was not the "man thing to do." During my upbringing, violence was promoted as the way we (as men) dealt with our problems. So when things got too complicated with the neighborhood gangs, I called my cousin, Juan, for backup.

Eventually, my involvement with the *Drifters* became more serious. When my parents thought that they had succeeded in moving me away from the gangs, the gangs came to me. At that time in my life, I had no sense of direction or purpose. All that mattered was feeling like I belonged to something. I was sixteen-years-old when I made a conscious decision to get "jumped" into the gang. The year was 1994, and I was initiated as a full-fledged gang member. After the initiation phase, my criminality progressed from stealing and fighting to actively hurting people. I would physically assault others just because of where they were from (or for any other reason that I thought would bring me status in my gang). I had become untouchable, or at least that is what I told myself. I did everything that gang members are known to do. My criminal activities progressed as I earned a reputation as a well-known and respected gang member. I had finally reached my cousin's status, but I was committed to surpass him.

I went to juvenile hall after using a gun to commit a robbery. My obsession with the gang culture intensified. Growing up with two older brothers and three older cousins, fighting was common. I used what I learned about fighting at home to continue building on my image while I was in juvenile hall. Fighting is all I really did there.

In 1996, I made the decision to act on my criminal beliefs, values, and emotions as I murdered a young man who did not deserve to die. I would love to undo the past (or be able to say that I made the decision to leave the gang culture after that tragedy and do what was right by my victim's memory), but that would be a lie.

In 1998, I entered the prison system after being sentenced to 16 years-to-life for my crime. My destination was Salinas Valley State Prison. It was my first time in prison, and I remember how it brought forth thoughts of hopelessness. The only way I saw myself leaving prison was in a casket. Whatever hope I once had was gone. Fear took the place of hope as I did not know what to expect. All I knew about prison was from what I had heard through stories. This fear was only enhanced after seeing two brutal stabbings just weeks into my incarceration. I was twenty-one, with a life sentence and I had no idea what life had in store for me. What I did know is that I refused to fall prey to anyone or anything. It was then that I remembered a saying I heard in the streets, "If you can't beat them, join them." That is the type of thinking I adopted in an attempt to justify my criminal actions.

From 1998 until 2011, I continued to involve myself in criminal activities, and I aligned myself with the Southerner prison gang. Because I was unwilling to be reformed, my incarceration did nothing to rehabilitate me. I wasn't confronting the poor choices that I had been making. I was afraid to see the real man in the mirror—the young man who had no regard for human life, not even his own. My beliefs were completely distorted, and based on my choices, what I valued most was a destructive lifestyle and the gang culture.

I remember a point in my life where I wanted (and needed) to stop hurting the people who mattered to me. I was tired of hurting people, and I was tired of hurting myself. I knew I needed to do something with my life, and I slowly began to understand that the lifestyle I was living was wrong. I needed to turn my life around, but I didn't see any way out of my criminal lifestyle. I wanted the tears to stop—and not only the tears of the people who were close to me, but also the tears of those who were affected by my actions. I was coming out of my denial, but I was unsure about what I needed to do.

I did not know what to do, but I knew that I needed to change my life. The problem was that I was still doing the devil's work. To break free from my bondage with the devil, I needed a power greater than myself. But who was powerful enough to overcome his hold on me? The answer had been there all along. The devil had already been defeated, and all I needed to do was surrender. For years, I heard people who cared about me say, "You need Jesus in your life." They were right.

In January of 2011, I had an unforgettable experience. For the first time, I understood how my actions devastated the lives of the people who had crossed my path. Some women visited the prison to share their experience of losing their sons to gang violence. The tears of the women had an effect on me that I cannot express with words. At that moment, I knew that my life would change. The women displayed amazing courage while sharing their suffering that took place because of cowards like me. This was the beginning of my spiritual awakening.

After that day, I began to do some serious soul searching. I became serious about my transformation. I wanted (and needed) to distance myself from criminals and that whole lifestyle. I needed a renewing of the mind. I needed to shift my beliefs. I needed to value people and myself. I began associating with people who could help me in my transformational process. I got involved with self-help groups, and I enrolled in our prison's substance abuse program as well. First, I was a participant, but I eventually worked my way up to become a peer mentor. This was where I found my purpose and my leadership abilities. In the midst of my transformation, I experienced a number of temptations. It seemed like the devil did not want to let go of me.

That same year, I was preparing all of the needed documents for my initial parole hearing (a hearing held for inmates like me who are serving a life sentence). The purpose of holding these hearings are to see if inmates are suitable for a second chance in society. On March 1, 2011, I was found suitable for parole. The parole commissioners saw the change in me; therefore, I would be afforded a second chance. I thought I was going home. However, five months and five days later, I received a letter from the Governor's office stating that Governor Brown elected to veto the Parole Board's decision.

Suddenly, home seemed far away. Nevertheless, I refused to give up. I could have thrown in the towel. Part of me wanted to, but I decided that this was an opportunity to show everyone, including myself, that my transformation was real. I looked into the reasons that the Governor used to reach his decision to deny my parole, and then I went back to work. Obstacles or setbacks would not determine my future and neither would my feelings of failure. Truthfully, I did feel like a failure. However, I learned that failure is never final, and it would be how I dealt with failure that would determine my path in life.

The devil wasn't finished tempting me. In 2012, eleven months after my initial parole hearing, I once again appeared before the Board of Parole Hearings (BPH) to see if I was suitable for parole. It took several hours for the commissioners to reach a decision. I remember hearing the words, "You are not suitable for parole," and then, "We believe that a five-year denial fits our decision." Imagine my thoughts and emotions; I was devastated. At that moment, all of the hope that I had was gone. I was visualizing the pain in the eyes of my wife, son, and mother. But then it dawned on me. What right did I have to feel victimized when I was the one who had victimized so many? I eventually realized that I deserved what I got. There were many things that I hadn't dealt with, and the commissioners made the right decision.

In Isaiah 41:10, the word of the Lord says, "Fear not for I am with you; be not dismayed, for I am your God. I will strengthen you, yes, I will help you, I will uphold you with my righteous right hand." These were the words God gave to me after my second BPH hearing, and they gave me the strength and comfort that only God could provide.

In February of 2012, I made the decision to push forward in life and not look back. It was also the year that I began to take my passion for helping others seriously. I began developing my leadership ability by becoming my brother's keeper within the Substance Abuse Program. I also pursued my education by working on my GED and simultaneously taking college courses through Palo Verde College so I could obtain certificates in the Alcohol and Drug Studies (ADS) field. I wanted to get more involved with my community and be an asset instead of a burden. I wanted to help others come out of their addictions. I have since accomplished all of those goals. I did get my GED, and I eventually earned my ADS Specialist I & II certificates. With my gang ties severed, I was looking forward to helping others find meaning and purpose for their lives. I did not let what happened in 2012 derail me. It was a crucible that I used as motivation to push forward and help others. I now understand that everything that happens in my life is for a purpose and that God's purpose will always supersede the devil's intention to bring me down.

I eventually made it to a Level 2 prison and life was good. I was comfortable, and the last thing I wanted was change. That is, however, exactly what happened when I was transferred to CTF-Soledad. Again, I was headed for the unknown. "God's purpose, not mine," were the words that I used to stay grounded. Even though this wasn't my first transfer, it was my first transfer where I would arrive at a new prison and announce that I had cut ties with my gang and would be living as a Christian. I really didn't know what to expect, but I had decided to entrust my life to God. It was a major step to take within the prison culture, and it was a pivotal transformational moment in my life. I understood the possible consequences, and I was spiritually at peace with the possibility of being ostracized (and even beaten) for what I believed in, since the only acceptance and recognition that I desired was from my family and God.

The word of the Lord says in Psalm 130:5, "I wait for the LORD, my soul waits, and in His word I do hope." The Lord speaks to all of us. At that time, I chose to view CTF-Soledad as a place of opportunity. It was at Soledad where I met a few good men (Rich, Ted, and Jason), men who helped me improve my leadership abilities. It was at Soledad where I was able to find a program that prepared me to take the exam to become a state certified Alcohol and Other Drug (AOD) counselor. Therefore, it was only due to my transfer to Soledad that I became a state certified AOD counselor. I have had many accomplishments since my transformation, that is, since I surrendered my life to God. I never thought that any of what has happened in my life was possible, especially how far along I have come with my education (considering that I only learned how to read and write in 2005). God is good. In my *True North* class, I learned that what happened in my life in 2012 was a crucible, a life-changing event. What I am discovering is that I am still in a crucible.

I believe that every goal I set is reachable. I believe that everything in life that is worth living for is worth fighting for. I know that life will knock me down from time to time, but it's up to me to get up, dust myself off, and answer the bell.

My transfer to Soledad and ensuing transformation are both blessings. Not only will I have a career when I parole, but I also have real friendships and a purpose in life. I plan to use my experience in prison and all that I have learned to reach those that many people have deemed unreachable. I will be God's vessel in helping the hopeless discover hope, and all of it started with the renewing of my mind.

Men Built for Others Profile

Name: Richie Reseda
Date of Birth: 10/24/91
Sentence: 10 years
Parole Eligibility: 2020

Leadership Maxim: *Every moment you're either making the world better or worse.*
Person He Is Most Inspired By: His wife, Taina Vargas-Edmond
Favorite Book: *The Will to Change: Men, Masculinity and Love* by Bell Hooks

Education & Interests
- Associate of Science in General Business
- Graduate of The Summer Youth Organizing Academy

Within our transformational community, Richie is a uniquely gifted leader and is at the forefront of transforming the culture of prison. He is one of the founders of an empowerment group for incarcerated youth called Success Stories. He also co-founded Initiate Justice, a nonprofit organization that is committed to building an evidence and community-based public safety system. He plays piano, raps, and has introduced intersectional politics to the prison environment. He is most proud that he has been married for four and a half years. What stands out more than all of Richie's accomplishments is that he walks the talk. He is a man of commitment and integrity, and he lives his life as a Man Built for Others.

Chapter 7

Man must evolve for all human conflict a method which rejects revenge, aggression and retaliation.
The foundation of such a method is love.

- Martin Luther King, Jr.

When I woke up, face down and handcuffed on that poor couple's damp lawn, my mind was both racing and blank. I was surprisingly calm for someone who had just committed a robbery and been tackled by a police officer. I could feel the cold barrel of the officer's gun pressed to the back of my head and his knee in my back. "I should've shot your a--!" he yelled. I wasn't panicked . . . I should have been.

As I spent the next few days alone in a cell awaiting arraignment, two things were on my mind. One was a continuous loop of action-movie-type fight scenes that I used as preparation for the altercations I'd soon be having in the county jail on behalf of my *hood*. The other thought was about how as soon as I got out of prison, I was going to finally focus 100% on my goal to improve global culture through media. At the time, the contradiction between these thoughts was lost on me.

My journey to become a nineteen-year-old pharmacy-robbing gang member with back-burner dreams of changing the world started some twelve years prior. As a child, I resented my disciplinarian father who worked two jobs and would come home to punish me harshly (and physically) for things I sometimes didn't do or even understand. I made up in my young mind that he, and by extension all authority, only sought to control and oppress me. When I entered a self-segregated middle school, where my working-class *biracialness* fit in with neither the rich and White or the Black and poor, I quickly gravitated towards the *gangsta* Black male media stereotype for acceptance. By age eleven, I was hanging out with gang members, and at twelve, I began smoking *weed*. At thirteen, I started selling it. I was addicted to the high, to the attention, and to the satisfaction of subverting authority.

I was fourteen when God sent me my first chance to escape my self-destructive irresponsibility. On a smoldering San Fernando Valley afternoon, I was sitting in my science class (part of a track of classes designed for failing students), when in walked two young counselors. One was a man with green eyes, gold skin, and a curly Afro. The other was a woman with tattooed, brown skin, and slim dreadlocks. As cool as they looked, I was not planning on listening to anything they had to say.

Over my friend's shoulder, I watched the man (whose name was Mark-Anthony) write the words MASS INCARCERATION on the whiteboard. He turned to the class and asked, "Who in here knows that they have a higher chance of going to prison than they do of going to college." Now they had my attention.

He and the other counselor, named Patrisse, would become my mentors. They taught me about addiction, recovery, and community organizing. They invited me to rallies and put me in positions of leadership. They offered me a new community-based identity that, for a time, I embraced. It was then that I decided to use my talent with art and music to solve community problems. Unfortunately, I never stopped using drugs, and a year and a half into my activism, I got addicted to ecstasy. I disappeared from the organizing world as fast as I came.

In the following years, my decision-making only got worse. I dropped out of school. My dad, who was tired of my behavior, kicked me out of the house when I was sixteen. I made my *homies* my family. I lived from place to place, and I began selling hard drugs. I partied daily. I stole, I manipulated, and I was arrested numerous times. I would still talk about my media dreams from time to time, but my actions revealed a life dedicated only to alcohol, drugs, and selfishness.

By the time I was sitting in jail for robbing the pharmacy, I was essentially three different people in one body. With my *homies*, I was a partier, a drug dealer (who used too much of his own supply), and someone who would do anything for attention. With my girlfriend (and friends from my organizing days), I was an artist who talked about promoting social justice. With my family, I was neither. In their eyes, I was quiet, disconnected, and distrusted. I never knew which character was my true self.

It was about a year into my sentence when I realized how compartmentalized my identity had become. After spending two months on lockdown with no phone access, I called my eighty-three-year-old grandmother from Folsom State Prison.

"WhassupNanna?!" I yelled excitedly.

"Why are you speaking to me that way?" she asked.

"What way?" I responded, faking confusion. Before the words even left my mouth, I realized I hadn't yet mentally code-switched out of my tough-guy, gang-member accent. At some point during that lockdown, I had decided that I was going to be one person, and that was a *gangsta*. I thought, *I don't have a choice. I'm going to live the next seven and a half years of my life in prison. Who else could I be?*

"You're talking to me like a guy in prison." Nanna's words woke me out of my daze. I felt embarrassed. I felt the sting of hearing criticism based on truth. I said nothing.

I didn't want to be a gang member anymore, but I was too scared to be anything else. My multiple-personality existence would have to continue.

I spent countless nights on my bunk trying to figure out how I could stay in the good graces of my peers while also avoiding the negativity that came along with it. Now, twenty years old with two strikes, I was aware that one act of violence could cost me a life sentence. On the other hand, so could the retaliation of other members if I didn't participate. In my cell, I read empowering and conscious authors like Bell Hooks and Michelle Alexander. On the yard, I did drugs and used the word "b--ch." The stratification of my identity was getting worse.

"F--- YOU B--CH A-- CRACKER!" The words rang down the hallway from the classroom next door. The racial slur got my attention. I was new to this medium-security prison, but my two years at a high-security facility (and my time in Los Angeles County Jail) taught me that language like that quickly led to violence. What scared me the most was that the voice was unequivocally Black. In the self-segregated world of California's prisons, that could potentially involve me and all of the other Black prisoners in whatever was going on.

At that time, I was two years into my incarceration, and I had found a sweet spot where I cunningly maintained respect from my homeboys while I also participated in college, self-help groups, and other programs oriented towards my goals. I had become comfortable with one foot pursuing my dreams and the other planted in the underworld. I had prayed that this moment wouldn't come—the moment where my willingness to be violent (and my dedication to the lifestyle) would be tested. I begged God for this not to happen.

But when I opened the door, no one was fighting. The only remnant of conflict was my homeboy breathing deeply as a correctional officer escorted him out of the building. My relief was short-lived... I knew this was not the end.

During our class break, my new friend, Charles, and I asked our friend (and my homeboy, G) what had happened next door in his class. Charles and G were both twenty-one, like me. The only difference was that Charles dedicated his life to Christianity, an acceptable way to give up the gang life within the prison culture. G, on the other hand, was very much active (criminally). He started telling Charles and I the story of how our *homie* got into an argument with their teacher. According to G, the teacher (a White man) had said something racist.

"The teacher is lucky the police came," G said in his ghetto accent. "As soon as the *homie* hit him, I would've jumped in!" His eyes were lit with excitement, which animated his tattooed face.

"WHAT?!" I exclaimed probably louder than I should have. I couldn't believe what I heard. G, whose release date was in a few months, had two strikes like me. Jumping a teacher would have earned him a third strike and a life sentence.

He scoffed, "You wouldn't do the same thing? You know the rules. One goes, we all go." My ears got hot. Certainly he couldn't be serious.

"Not on a teacher! You'll get life!" I both demanded and pleaded. G squinted his eyes, making him look both suspicious and devious.

He looked at me and said, "It don't matter, bro. That's the code. If you ain't willing to do life for this sh-t, then what are you doing it for?" He was serious. A small, scared voice in my head told me to shut up before I blew my cover. I didn't.

"I would never throw my life away for no stupid sh-t like that," I said indignantly. I was furious. G looked at me with confusion and disgust.

"If someone walked in here with a *burner* (pistol) right now," he said, never breaking eye contact, "lined us up, and asked who in here is willing to die for their hood . . . I would kneel down in front of the gun." He ended his performance on his knees, arms spread wide in a dramatic pose. Charles laughed nervously. *What have I gotten myself into?* I thought.

In the following days, I noticed a weird energy when I came around the *homies*. Some didn't even make eye contact with me when we shook hands. *G is my friend*, I thought. *I know he didn't tell them what I said.*

I talked to Charles about it. "You don't think he told them what I said, do you?" I felt ridiculous asking that question. *What I said was rational. Jumping a teacher is wrong! Jumping a teacher is dumb! I have a future! I just got married!*

"You need to draw your line in the sand," Charles told me. "Are you gonna live for the gang or go home to your wife and do this music?"

He spoke with more reason than I wanted to hear. When I spoke to my wife, Taina, about it, she told me the same thing. *Easy for them to say*, I thought. *Charles is Christian, and Taina has never lived this.* I was stuck.

One night, it became apparent that G had told everyone what I said.

"Tomorrow night, we gonna have a meeting," said the unofficial leader of our group. "All the real *homies* are invited." His tone told me what the meeting was going to be about. I had a decision to make.

That night on my bunk, I ran the scenario over and over in my head . . . the exchange with G in the hallway . . . the conversations with Taina and Charles. *I should go there tomorrow and fight all of them*, I thought. *Or maybe this is my opportunity to leave this life alone.* I measured the risks and rewards of every possible outcome. I kept thinking about how I needed to get out of prison to Taina and eliminate this kind of culture. I felt anxious.

When it came time to go to the yard the next day, I didn't know what I was going to do. I felt fear for what the *homies* might do to me, but I also felt sorrow for them. I lamented the fact that this was what our lives had become. I watched them group up across the yard. *What a sad waste of human potential*, I thought.

I should beat G's a-- for running and telling them what I said. My legs started walking towards them. *If I tell them I'm done, they're gonna jump me and I'll lose my release date anyways.* I was about ten feet away. *If that happens, at least I lost it for something . . .*

I stopped in front of them. They stared awkwardly.

"I'm done." I couldn't believe my own mouth. I couldn't stop it either.

"This is dumb. I'm done."

"With gang banging?!" a *homie* with an astonished face and a tattoo between his eyes asked.

"With all of it," I replied. G stood up. I balled my fists. The leader got up, too. I clenched my jaw. There was silence.

"That's what I'm talking about," G said with a wide smile. He opened up his arms with his dramatic pose. This time, he hugged me. The leader stuck out his hand for a handshake.

"I respect you as a man," he said.

As a result of the decision I made that day, and the overwhelming support from Taina, my family, my mentors, and an amazing community of friends (both inside and outside of prison), I am living an integrated life. I am drug, alcohol, gang, and crime free. I have fully embraced my goals, and I live them out daily.

I have released an album from prison that criticizes violent culture with wit. I have achieved an Associate of Arts degree in Business. Charles and I co-founded a self-improvement program for incarcerated youth. I've contributed writings to multiple publications and have received a job offer as a content contributor for a social impact magazine. Taina and I have started a public safety policy nonprofit organization.

Most importantly, today, I am one person. I am defined by my relationship with God who leads me to use my talents to love people and invest in my community. I am five years into an eight-and-a-half-year sentence, and I am truly free.

Men Built for Others Profile

Name: Patrick Griffin
Date of Birth: 8/17/57
Sentence: 25 years-to-life
Parole Eligibility: 2018

Leadership Maxim: *The least among you shall be the greatest.*
Person He Is Most Inspired By: The Apostle Paul, Martin Luther, and his wife
Favorite Book: *Charity and its Fruits* by Jonathon Edwards

Education & Interests
- GED
- Author of five published books

Patrick has been in prison longer than any other person in this book (over 35 years). In spite of the length of his prison term, he is best known for being a Christian who takes seriously the call of God on his life. We have come to know him as a man of God, a deep thinker, a non-fiction writer, and a teacher. In April of 2017, he will celebrate his anniversary with his wife of three years, Donnalee. Patrick is a man who diligently strives to please God by honoring His Son, Jesus Christ. He is a man who strives to love others as Christ loves him, and through his diligence, Patrick lives his life as a Man Built for Others.

Chapter 8

Seek ye first the kingdom of God, and His righteousness; and all these things shall be added unto you.

Matthew 6:33, King James Version

I am a 59-year-old prisoner, who has been incarcerated in California since the age of twenty-one. My good father, Patrick Sr., who was a hard-working pipe-liner devoted to his family, placed his name on me the day I was born. After me, came a brother and two sisters (for a stable family of six) who drove about our middle-class world in a Ford station wagon.

From my supportive home, I went to well-funded schools with teachers eager to facilitate development in any student showing interest. The neighborhood crime rate was extremely low with no significant gang problem. I did okay with grades, but the focus for me was athletics and pursuing my dream of playing professional baseball. Every night, I listened to the play-by-play games of the Dodgers and Angels. A typical day for me was playing pick-up ball with friends, practicing my batting swing in front of a window, or throwing a hardball repeatedly into a brick wall and fielding the bounce-back. Almost every boy my age could run faster, throw harder, and hit the ball farther than I could, but I held on to the dream and worked hard.

During my freshman year of high school, I practiced after class for months with the boys who hoped to make the roster on the varsity, junior-varsity, or freshman-sophomore team. One day in early March, I walked into the locker room and saw the rosters posted on a wall near the equipment cage. My name was on none of them.

Standing in front of that wall with those papers looking back at me, I felt sad and ridiculous. For years, I had made it known to my family, friends, and classmates that my future was baseball. I was known as the kid who always wanted to "talk baseball." But now, with those rosters staring at me, I mentally said to myself, "You couldn't even make the freshman team. What a joke!"

When I left the locker room, I was aware of the difference in my mood and outlook. I told myself something like, "All of these years you chased a ridiculous idea. You worked so hard and dreamed so big, but the joke is on you." It was time to read the road sign in my life, which showed that my future was not in athletics. So what might it be? Wisdom would have instructed me to talk with my parents, teachers, and the freshman counselor. I should have felt grateful for the years of fun that I spent hanging out on a baseball diamond and then focused on realistic goals for the life in front of me. Instead, I interpreted the roster experience as a failure that defined me, and I used it as an excuse to give up.

At school, I started pulling away from my normal crowd and hanging out with kids who used drugs and expressed a more rebellious attitude. I grew my hair as long as my parents would allow, started ditching school, and listening to music that promoted the drug and rebellious culture of the late 60s and early 70s. One Saturday afternoon, about a month after the roster experience, I was walking through a field with two other boys my age. We stopped under a large tree, where one of the boys pulled out a joint, lit it up, and passed it around. I remember watching how they dragged on the joint and held in the smoke as long as they could, and I did my best to imitate what I was seeing. That was my first time getting high. I remember looking around at the field, the nearby street, the shopping center, and then mentally saying, "This is me."

I felt that I had found my place in life and that I was becoming a part of something new, strong, and meaningful. In my interpretation of things, I was joining up with "cool" people like Ozzy Osborne, Jimi Hendrix, and Timothy Leary. I had acceptance with a new crowd of friends, and I was making the statement that my parents did not have as much authority over me as they thought. I would live by my own rules, choose my own values, have as much fun as I could, and do whatever I could get away with.

I didn't realize it then, but on that day while standing under the tree, I made a mental and social turn from a life that was centered in my home to a life set adrift. I had chosen a wrong answer in my search for self-identity and for the place where I fit in.

From marijuana, I advanced to other experiments with drugs such as LSD, PCP, amphetamines, and barbiturates. Other than marijuana, I did not seek out those drugs or use them regularly, but if they were available, I did not hesitate to indulge. More than the feeling of being high, I was stimulated by the feeling of doing what was acceptable and cool among the crowd I now identified with.

In choosing to ingest mind-altering drugs (and by that, I include marijuana), I was taking into my psyche so much more than I understood at the time. For me, using drugs was like taking on a magical view of life. It was like putting on glasses that changed the shape of what was really there. Like the kids today who absurdly glamorize the *gangsta* lifestyle, I glamorized the drugs and the music that went with it. The price I paid was an increasing collapse of motivation to put in the work of building and holding onto the values that would give shape to a responsible lifestyle. The use of illicit drugs does not affect every user the way it did me, but I know that in my own experience, the use of mind-altering substances contributed powerfully to my collapse as a morally responsible person.

My parents saw up close the negative change in their son whom they loved and so deeply cared for. They would have committed themselves and their resources to any positive pursuit I might have expressed interest in, and they tried to stir my interest in positive ideas such as planning for college. I hurt them badly by my failing grades and by showing less and less interest in my siblings who looked up to me as the oldest. Looking back, I can hardly describe how awful I feel for how I disappointed and grieved my family.

I dropped out of high school my senior year. With no positive values to regulate my choices, my goals, or my vision for what I might do with the life I'd been given, I lacked the motivation to go back to school or to maintain a job. In 1975, at the age of 18, I robbed a store for a small sum of money and was arrested. I served about 17 months in the Youth Authority (YA), and I came out worse than I was before I went in (much worse). My lack of a stable self-image left me vulnerable to the extreme criminalizing influences of jail and prison. In that culture, it was an insult to be called a civilian. It was cool to be a convict.

After my release from YA, I tried living at home and forming friendships with positive people. However, I quickly realized that I felt more comfortable with people who had experienced the jailhouse and those who absorbed its culture. I met an ex-con named Jimbo, and he became my "road dog." Through Jimbo, I came into contact with a lot of ex-cons, and being around those influences reinforced my self-image as a loser and a reject. Honestly, when I was around successful people, I felt out of place. I only felt genuine in the company of those I regarded as losers and rebels like myself.

I shifted from marijuana to alcohol because it energized me socially and emboldened me in barrooms and at parties. I mostly stayed away from crime, and I lived off of my income. Then, in early 1979, I began to feel the deep embarrassment of a failed life. I had turned twenty-one, and I knew my lifestyle was disgraceful, but I didn't believe I was capable of initiating and sustaining anything positive. My parents were still trying to reach out to me, but I wasn't motivated, and I turned more heavily to alcohol. In April, I stopped showing up for work and began doing small burglaries at places of business.

This dark and dangerous outlook eventually culminated in me shooting one of my friends over a petty argument and then shooting an officer who attempted to arrest me for the crime. Both of these men survived, and because the sentencing laws in the 1970s were extremely lenient by today's standards, I was offered a package deal. I pleaded guilty to two counts of assault with a deadly weapon and received a combined sentence of eight years. That could seem unbelievable to someone growing up in today's sentencing culture. But in those times, unless a victim died, the sentence was determinate and there were no enhancements or priors. Today, each of those crimes would carry a life sentence. But in 1979, when I came into the California Department of Corrections and Rehabilitation (CDCR), I was told that with good time/work time credits, my earliest release date would be February 1, 1984. This meant that I could be released from prison at the age twenty-six if I stayed out of trouble . . . I didn't stay out of trouble.

During my first two years, I picked up three new cases for violence that involved the use of weapons. I received the additional sentences of seven years, three years, and twenty-five years-to-life. The life sentence was for murdering another inmate in March of 1981.

By that time, my life was totally out of control. Although I was never a gang member, I had absorbed the gangster culture and took much pride in being recognized as a solid *peckerwood*. (*Peckerwood* is a word that Blacks once used as a derogatory term for Whites, very much like the "N" word used derogatorily against Blacks. Over time, Whites in prison internalized the word and began taking pride in being called "a good *peckerwood*.")

I really wasn't "solid," but I had a good front. One way to get respect in prison is to be perceived as dangerous. To be called "a killer" is a high compliment in the perverse culture of prison. So that was the one thing I had accomplished in life. I was a "killer" who was recognized by my peers as a "righteous convict." That's how small my world had become. My mind had imploded to a singularity of ignorance. There were no longer any competing forces within me. I had given myself entirely to the role of being a "convict," and my daily experience was a desperate effort to hide from the reality of a failed life. I wore a face that said, "I'm not worried about anything. I don't give a f--k." That's how prisoners disguise their deep sense of failure, shame, and fear—they wear a mask of arrogance.

I had gotten good at playing that role, and whenever I began to feel depressed, I would flush it out with rage. I blamed others for where I was and how I had failed. It was like my mind was running as fast as it could to not let reality catch up. By reality, I mean the awareness that I had no one to blame but myself. I was a selfish and greedy person who had caused enormous pain and loss in the lives of others, including my own family who loved me and who were baffled at how I had become the person I was.

One night, in June of 1981 (three months after the murder), I received a letter from the eldest of my two younger sisters. She said my family was requesting that I no longer write to my youngest sister because of concerns that I was being a bad influence on her. Hearing those words from my family cut through everything. I set the letter on my bunk and started pacing while smoking Camel cigarettes. I was telling myself, "My own family is pulling away from me—I've become that ugly." I couldn't shake the depression. For the first time, I could no longer find within myself the ability to point a finger at somebody else.

When the guards came by with dinner, I waved them off. After dinner, the tier would always be noisy with guys at their bars yelling out to each other, capping on each other, and swapping war stories. It seemed to me that they were animals who were happy because they just got fed. Normally, I would have been contributing to the noise, but that night I stayed quiet. Someone called out to me, "Hey Patrick, what's up?" He said this because I was being quiet, so I answered, "I'm not feeling good tonight." That took care of it. Everyone went on with the usual, and I just kept pacing and smoking Camels.

That night, when the lights went out and the tier fell quiet, I sat on my bunk by the bars and looked out at the wall on the other side of the catwalk. I remember wrapping a hand around one of the bars and tugging it. I stared at the bar and thought about what kind of person would need to be locked in a cage with no way out.

I was given a good life. My parents were not perfect, but they provided a stable home where my childhood environment was safe and nurturing. So much had been given to me, and society had then given me a second chance after my teenage incarceration for robbery. But I had managed to lose everything, and I damaged the happiness and welfare of many others along the way. So that night, while I was in my cell, I began looking around at what was left: a toilet, a sink, a tiny room, and the smell of steel and cement. Then I looked up at the vent, and I knew immediately that I would hang myself.

Without getting off of the bunk, I lit a cigarette and looked over at the letter from my sister that was still open and laying on my blanket. After a minute, I stood, tossed the cigarette in the toilet, placed my sister's letter in a little box of personal items, and then pulled a sheet off of my bed to make a noose.

Nobody could see what I was doing. There was no one to stop me, and in my mind, I was not second-guessing. There was no back-and-forth of whether I should do it or not. It was time to die, and there was no other thought. In the shadows at the back of my cell, I stood by the toilet and fashioned the noose. But I never made it up to the vent. After twisting the sheet into a hangman's rope, the next thing I distinctly remember is being down on my knees with my face pressed to the floor, and the only concern in my mind was an awareness of God. I don't remember how that came about. I just remember it was there. I was overwhelmed with a sudden awareness that I was guilty, filthy, and deserving of nothing but condemnation. It no longer mattered that I was in prison or that my life was destroyed. It only mattered that I was guilty and condemned in the sight of God.

I don't know how long I stayed on the floor like that. It could have been minutes, or it could have been an hour. But at some point, a new thought took hold, and it came with a powerful emotion. Although I could not have articulated it intellectually at that time, I suddenly believed that all of my problems with God and with life were resolved in Jesus Christ.

Down on the floor with no one else in the world knowing what was going on in my cell, I felt a peace that came with the name Jesus Christ. I remember opening my eyes and being aware of the soft yellow glow of light from the catwalk filtering in through the bars. The soft light seemed so very peaceful. I knew that something inside of me had changed, and I knew that I would not hang myself and that my life would be different from that point.

I got up from the floor and made my bed, then climbed in and fell asleep between those same sheets that I had intended to use for hanging. When I woke up in the morning, the peace I felt the night before was still there. During the day, I located a Bible (I don't remember how I got it). As I started reading, I felt the voice of God speaking to me in what I read. I was twenty-three-years-old and full of energy. I read all day, and the day after that, and the day after that. The excitement of learning about Christ, what God had done for me, and what I had inherited by believing the Gospel took hold of my mind with a powerful fascination. At one point, I remember pausing after having paced back and forth for a long time with the open Bible in my hands. I reflected on how differently I felt about myself, about others, and about life itself. It seemed I had been snatched out of one realm and placed into another. Everything looked differently, sounded differently, and felt differently.

A few days after my transformational experience of faith, the correctional officers were running showers, and as usual, they would let us out one at a time. One of the guys who lived on my tier was on a social ban that we called "the shine." I don't remember what he had done, but no one from my race was supposed to talk to or interact with him in any way. His name was Calvin. As he passed in front of my cell on his way to the shower, I looked at him and felt compassion. I said, "Hey Calvin." He stopped and said, "Yeah, what's up?" I said, "Do you need some shampoo?" He said, "Yeah." I put a bottle of shampoo on the bars. He would not come near my cell, so I stepped back. When he saw that it was safe, he stepped up, took the bottle, and said, "Hey, thanks, Pat." As he walked away, one of the guys who lived a few cells away called out to me with a challenge, saying, "Hey, Pat, what's up?" I said to him, "Whatever you want to be up." When I said that, I realized I had just served notice that what had previously been expected of me should no longer be expected.

I felt elated and energized by what I had just done, and I consciously felt a release from the public act that I had played for so long. It seemed to me that after having become an animal, I was now a human being, and I wasn't going to let anyone take that away. So basically, what I said to my peers on that day was, "What I'm into now, don't mess with it. This is me, and don't expect anything else." From that day, I have never identified myself as representing anything except Jesus Christ.

Since my experience of faith, I now have more than 35 consecutive years without a rule violation in prison. In 2009, I was noticed by a former Director of the CDCR, Jim Rowland, who has visited and written me numerous times (Mr. Rowland is the Director who oversaw the building of the Security Housing Units in the late 1980s and did much to bring down violence in California's prisons). For my parole hearings, I receive support letters from Mr. Rowland, from a former CDCR Captain named Ed George, from other persons who have backgrounds in law enforcement, as well as from family and friends. I have also received laudatory chronos from officers here in the prison. After a horrific start with my first two years in the system, I have now lived productively and peacefully while maintaining full-privilege status for more than three decades (with no relapse into the use of alcohol or drugs—both of which are readily available).

By the grace of God, and through my faith, I have experienced the motivation to not turn back even in the worst of times. And there have been rough times. In 2002, I was called to the counselor's office and told that my mom had died. Just like that, she had a brain aneurysm. Except for seeing me in visiting rooms and talking to me on the phone, she never got to see how profoundly and completely her son had become a different person in positive ways. It was hard to come to grips with a world in which Mom isn't here anymore. I cried like a baby, and I didn't care who might come by my cell and see. Not only was there the agony of losing Mom, but also the grief of being unable to stand with my family during such a time. While my family buried my mom, I (the oldest son), was sitting in prison.

My closest outside friend is Fred Mendrin, who paroled in 1985 and now works for what is called Prison Fellowship. Fred had come to prison in 1970 for possession of a half-an-ounce of marijuana. But he joined a prison gang and earned a life sentence for a gang-related murder while living in a section of Chino called Palm Hall. In 1978, he experienced Christ by faith and became a dramatically different person on that day. I met Fred in 1982, and for his last three years in the system, I served with him in the ministry. Since his parole, he has not only stayed in touch, but he has been involved with the details of my life. I rarely go a week without calling Fred, and he has even visited me in prison (where we've watched each other grow old in the face but new in the spirit). I have watched his daughters grow up in visiting rooms, and his wife is a delightful and supportive friend. So, in 2002, after receiving the news that my mom had died, I called Fred (at his home in Fresno) and asked him to stand with my family in my place at the funeral. That same night, he was on the road, driving several hundred miles from Fresno to Anaheim to be with my family.

After the funeral, in a large room with tables for all who had attended, my dad gave Fred a seat beside him at the table reserved for immediate family members. He was recognized as being there in my place, and to this day, my family regards him highly for such an act of friendship. Prior to my transformation, there is no friend who would have respected me enough to make such a sacrifice, nor would I have been able to build a close friendship with a person of such character.

Losing Mom was a hard experience that only drew me deeper into my transformational relationship with Christ. I stayed focused and positive, believing that God will create ways to honor His name in my life and for me to honor my mom just as if she was here to see it. He blessed my efforts at research and writing. I have five published books, three of which were published by a company formed by my sister and named after our mom ("The Mary Ellen Group"). Also, this is the sister who wrote me that letter in 1981.

In every prison where I have been housed, I have worked in chapels, been involved in ministry, and built strong and lasting friendships. But most of all, about three years ago, the Lord who gave meaning to my life when I had lost everything, created an astonishing miracle that only increases in beauty with the passing of time. It started with me going for a walk one sunny day on the yard in March of 2013. While passing by the phone area, I saw a friend named Stefan waving for me. I turned aside to see what he wanted, and little did I know that my life was about to change in a wonderful and dream-like way.

As I got near to the phone area, Stefan said, "Hey, my friend, Donnalee, has a question about the Bible. Do you think you could help her?" I took the phone and spoke (for the first time) with the woman who a year later would move to Soledad and marry me. She now lives only three miles from the prison, and she visits nearly every available visiting day while being used by Christ to change the shape of my life in ways that I could not have imagined.

What drew Donnalee to me was only one thing. When I answered her question about the Bible and spoke with her about Christ, she sensed a sincerity of love and faith. She believed that her God had brought her to the man who would be the Christian husband that she always wanted. That such a woman could be drawn to me shows more than anything else how Christ has transformed me. Her presence inspired me to push even more into a life that honors Christ and is regulated by the values that I have learned in Him.

When my wife is with me on weekends, I'm like a little boy on Christmas morning—holding her hand with an open Bible in front of us, sharing food, praying, singing, and talking about our vision and faith toward the future. Often, when I'm looking into her eyes, I flash back on where I've come from and how impossible this all would have seemed. For so many years, for decades, I did not expect that such a blessing was possible in my life. My dream is to serve in the outside community with my wife at my side. I want to comfort and meet the needs of hurting people in the name of the Lord, for He is the one who took the ruins of my soul and my life and made all things new.

Men Built for Others Profile

Name: Arcadio Acuna
Date of Birth: 10/26/51
Sentence: Life + Life + Life + 8 years
Parole Eligibility: 2017

Leadership Maxim: *Serving God by being of service to others.*
Person He Is Most Inspired By: His Lord and Savior, Jesus Christ
Favorite Book: The Bible

Education & Interests
- High School Graduate, Alta Loma High, 1969
- Alcohol & Drug Studies (Specialist I)

Arcadio's transformation is radical. He went from surviving 20 years in the Pelican Bay Security Housing Unit (SHU) for his association with a prison gang, to devoting himself to helping others. He just received a three-year sobriety chip and was the opening speaker for the first ever three-day recovery conference held inside a state prison. Today, he sponsors other men in their recovery, he is a man of prayer, and he asks God daily for strength and guidance to live a godly life. At the age of 65, he is committed to helping people stay away from alcohol and drugs and to take their sobriety one day at a time. Through his service and commitment to loving his neighbor, Arcadio lives his life as a Man Built for Others.

Chapter 9

¡Si se puede!

- Cesar Chavez

My name is Arcadio Acuna, and I was born on October 26, 1951, in the north town barrio of a small town called Cucamonga. My family was very poor. However, because we always had enough to eat and new clothes to wear on the first day of school, I did not realize how poor we were until later. I do not know how we did it because my dad only made $80 a week while working as the bottling-room foreman at one of the local wineries. I recall that my childhood was a happy one, and my father was known as the "fun" dad of the neighborhood. All of my friends liked to hang out at my house because of the mini-bikes and other motorized toys that my dad taught us how to build and maintain.

While growing up, I always knew that my father's word was the law of the house and that he alone made the important decisions concerning the day-to-day life of our small family. He ruled over his small kingdom with an iron hand, showing me and my three brothers an outstanding work ethic that I still carry with me to this day. He also showed us that being the man of the house meant taking care of the family by any means necessary, even if those means were violent. On numerous occasions, I saw him use violence and physical force when he saw anyone threatening or disrespecting his family in any way.

My father also exposed us to a distorted machismo point of view concerning relationships with the opposite sex. From an early age, he showed us that a man was allowed to be unfaithful to his wife or girlfriend, and he was supposed to have sex with as many women as possible. As strange as it was, I noticed that his distorted way of thinking was tolerated by the females in our close-knit community.

My father's dominance over household affairs even went as far as making the decisions about what we ate for dinner when he came home from work. Having been born on a ranch in the northern state of Zacatecas, Mexico, he would not allow any form of fish to be served at his table. My mother, Josephine, on the other hand, was from the state of Jalisco, where seafood was one of the main staples in almost every home. This meant that if she wanted to eat fish, then she had to prepare it separately and eat it away from the table by herself.

Even with all of the ups and downs, my family had what it needed. But my whole life changed in the blink of an eye when on April 28, 1961, my mother died from a cancer. The disease came on so quickly that we did not even have time to adjust to her being sick. In a matter of days, life changed for our family. And my father, who had been the hardest worker I had ever known, turned into a stone-cold alcoholic who stayed dead drunk for the next twenty years of his life.

A couple of events compounded the effects of my mother's death. On the bus ride home from a weeklong camping trip in the San Bernardino Mountains, one of my classmates said something about my mom having cancer. Being the wise-mouth that I was (and sometimes still am), I made an off-hand remark about liking it when she was sick because she gave me money and stuff to make me happy. When I got home from that camping trip, I found that my mother had been taken to the City of Hope Hospital. A few days later, she would quickly die.

Additionally, my older half-brother told me that he overheard my mom tell her doctor that she had a son who made her sick. I don't know if she really said that or not, but it was always in the back of my mind, and it affected me deeply from that point forward.

My mother was the center of my life. She was the core that held our family together, and her loss shook our family to its very foundation. When she died, my soul ached, and I could not shake the guilt for what I had said. Moreover, I could not rid myself of the memory of what my brother had said. I began to feel that I was so naturally evil that God had decided to punish me by killing my mother.

Being the oldest son, I felt compelled to take over the responsibilities of the family. I decided that from that day forward, I was going to look after my two younger brothers and my alcoholic father.

Despite my guilt, life went on. Without my mother, it was a struggle to make sure there was food in the house to feed my brothers and father. I took on the chore of running our household—washing and ironing clothes; cleaning the house; and seeing that the water, gas, and light bills were paid on time. In truth, the duties that I took on kept me from hanging out on the corner with the homeboys, and I believe that is what kept me from getting into trouble with the law (the way that so many others did when we were teenagers).

In fact, I hated being at home so much that I stayed in school as long as I could, and I played every after-school sport there was just to avoid returning home. To give a better picture of what my life was like in those days, imagine living in a house being run by an alcoholic father, with three young boys who had no rules to follow, and no one to give us direction on what we could or could not do. My home was like the "Animal House," where every sort of misbehavior and crime happened. My home was where runaways came to stay and where alcohol and drug users came to get high and do dope deals. My home was a haven for criminality.

I continued going to school and did fairly well in classes. I was good in sports, played football, and was on the track team. I learned to play the trumpet, was a member of the school band, and even got to march in a few parades dressed in one of those fancy uniforms. I was good enough at playing football that I was offered a scholarship to attend one of the Claremont Colleges.

I found it easy to make friends, and I would often visit the guys I played sports with at their homes. This is when I first began to notice how poor my family was. The homes that I visited made mine look like a broken-down shack. They had swimming pools, pianos in their living rooms, and my friends had lots of money to spend on new clothes, bicycles, and an assortment of other stuff I could only dream of having.

I distinctly remember that I was so embarrassed of the house I lived in that I would never invite any of my school friends over to visit. I started feeling like there was something innately wrong with me. I believed that God had chosen to punish me by killing my mother, allowing my dad to turn into a wino, and causing my family to live in abject poverty because of the evil nature I had been born with. I grew to hate this God that my mother had once taught me was loving and merciful.

I don't know how, but in spite of all this, I was able to graduate from high school. I married my childhood sweetheart, went to work to support my newborn son (Mark), and moved from my house in the barrio to my own apartment in Ontario. Of course, I still had to take care of and look after my brothers and father. So at nineteen, I was responsible for the welfare of two separate families. This obligation kept me from going to Vietnam in the early '70s—and perhaps saved my life because so many of my football buddies went over there and never came back.

In 1970, I went to work in the shipping department of a large manufacturing company called Philips Industries. It only took me six months to work my way into a lead-man position, thanks to the work ethic my father had taught me as a kid. Within a year, I was promoted to shipping supervisor, and in four short years, I rose up to become the company's Traffic Manager who was responsible for the shipping, warehouse, and fleet departments. For some reason, the owner of the company took a real liking to me and ended up making me the youngest department head the company ever had. I was the highest paid employee—and the only Hispanic to hold such an administrative position.

In this job, I became what is sometimes referred to as a "functional alcoholic." It seemed to me as if drinking alcohol was a job requirement. We all ate lunch together, had mixed drinks with our food, frequented the local watering holes every day after work for Happy Hour, and had poker night every Friday at one of the fellas' houses where we often got stinking drunk. I do not know how many times I drove home so drunk that I couldn't see straight, and it is only by the grace of God that I never crashed the car and killed myself or somebody else.

I also found that once I became the Traffic Manager, the distorted belief system and criminal mentality I had brought with me into adulthood was actually rewarded. I was encouraged to cheat both our vendors and our customers. Moreover, because I was given a budget to work within, I even cheated and stole from those who worked under me so that at the end of the year I would get a bonus.

In the end, I was fired. While hung-over, and in a fit of rage, I assaulted the general manager after he embarrassed me in front of a young female worker whom I was trying to seduce. Needless to say, my fairytale life came crashing down around me. By this time, I had separated from my second wife after she caught me cheating with one of her best friends in our own bed. Making matters worse, she found out that I had fathered a child with another woman while we were married. After we broke up, I went back to live in the barrio with my brothers and dad. This is when I dove into the criminal life in a big, big way.

After I was fired, I received a large sum of money for the vacations that I never took and the profit sharing the company had been putting away for my retirement. Since my two kid brothers had become heroin addicts, we decided that I should use all of my money to buy a large quantity of heroin. In our criminally distorted thinking, the plan would result in all of us becoming extremely wealthy.

Needless to say, things did not go exactly as we thought they would. I became viciously addicted to heroin, and in a short time, I developed a $400-a-day habit. I resorted to committing every imaginable crime to support my insatiable habit, and in about one year, I was arrested for the first time in my life and sent to prison. The year was 1977.

Today, after having served more than thirty years for a string of crimes that I committed in 1985, I have since spent almost twenty years in the Security Housing Unit (SHU) of Pelican Bay State Prison for being validated as an associate of a prison gang. After many years of denial, I finally admitted that I deserved to be in the SHU, and I earned the CDCR's label of the "worst of the worst."

I spent much of my time as a so-called "jailhouse lawyer" who challenged the conditions of the SHU as being in violation of the 8th Amendment's prohibition against cruel and unusual punishment. Doing this gave me the opportunity to learn about the long-term effects of sensory deprivation on a person's psychological and physiological well-being. I also discovered how the techniques used in the SHU were first applied on American prisoners-of-war during the Korean Conflict as a means to brainwash them and break their spirits so that they would speak out against the U.S. government. I also saw firsthand what these techniques did to prisoners when, during the first few years after the SHU was opened, there were a rash of suicides. Sadly, I witnessed more than a few of my friends begin to show signs of mental illness.

I also felt the effects of this forced isolation when I became sensitive to light and sound. I began to prefer living in total darkness, and I would get uncontrollably angry just from hearing others talk over the tier from cell to cell. On numerous occasions, I noticed that when I left my unit (while handcuffed and under escort), it was hard for me to breathe, and I experienced a sense of distorted perception. When walking down a long corridor, it actually seemed to me that objects were moving away from me instead of getting closer. But, by far, the event that impacted me the most and took me to the lowest point in my life was when one of my dearest and closest friends passed away while we were in the SHU.

I am referring to my pal, Juan (Tito) Ortiz. Here was a man who was almost fifty years old and had come into the prison system at the age of seventeen. Because he had a learning disability and could not read or write very well, he had lost touch with his family. He had not received a letter from home for the last ten years of his life.

One day, during an institutional count, they saw that he was lying on the floor of his cell and not moving. Because SHU protocol did not allow for staff to open a door unless a prisoner is securely handcuffed, it took a long time to get him out of the cell, and a few hours more to transport him to an outside hospital. By the time he got there, he had slipped into a coma from liver failure. Not long after, he quietly died. It broke my heart to find out that he had passed. Since he had not provided the department with his family's contact information, they could not be notified of his death. I was told that his body was donated to some university to be cut up and used in whatever way they use unclaimed cadavers. To this day, I still do not know if his family ever found out that he died.

I have to confess that after my friend's death, I sank into a state of utter hopelessness and despair. I began thinking that someday I was going to die in the same way—a lonely old man, forgotten and forsaken by family and friends, living out his days in a world without love. I feared that when I died, nobody was even going to notice (or even care).

It was during this time of spiritual and emotional crisis that I decided to turn my will and my life over to the care of God. I made up my mind that even if I had to spend the rest of my life in the SHU, I was going to make the most out of it. I decided to try and be the best person I could be. Now, I cannot honestly say that I went through an epiphany or that I felt a bolt of lightning hit me or anything like that. But little by little, I started to feel a kind of peace come into my heart, and I realized that I never had to feel alone again. I think the biggest transformation for me was my change in attitude. Rather than look for what the world had to give me, I started to think of ways I could be of service to others. I also began to truly believe there was hope for a better future.

I went back to exercising strenuously to maintain the best physical conditioning possible. My thirst for knowledge seemed to grow in leaps and bounds as I read every book I could get my hands on, and I started small study groups with other prisoners. I prayed every day, faithfully read my Bible, and I studied

God's word through several correspondence courses in order to strengthen my relationship with my loving God.

In September of 2011, during the middle of our second hunger strike in protest of the conditions in which we were forced to live, I was taken to a classification committee hearing. I was granted inactive gang status and released back into the general population. After initially being sent to a Level 4 yard, it was only by the mercy and grace of God that fourteen months later I was transferred to a Level 2 prison (CTF-Soledad). This is where so many opportunities for positive programming and personal growth opened up to me.

I have taken advantage of most of them. I vigorously embraced the Twelve Steps of Alcoholics Anonymous, and I was chosen to be the lead speaker for the first ever three-day AA conference held in a prison. I enrolled in college to earn my certification as an Alcohol and Drug Specialist, and I have a job waiting for me as a drug counselor for the House of Hope Christian half-way house when the lord decides to grant me my return to the community.

As of this writing, I am waiting to go before the parole board on March 23, 2017, for consideration for release on parole. I know that it is only by the grace of God that after spending so many years in solitary confinement I am strong in body, mind, and spirit. At sixty-five years of age, after having spent more than thirty years in prison, I am filled with hopes and dreams of a bright future. I firmly believe that God brought me to this exact place at this exact moment for a reason. I do not yet know what that reason is. Maybe it's to right an injustice that was done by the judicial system to someone through the law work that I do. Or perhaps by hearing my story, someone will make a commitment to be a responsible, sober, and drug-free son of God. I pray that by my example, someone will find the peace of mind that comes from the transformation that I have experienced and that they can begin to live with the kind of hope that will allow them to face a future that holds the promise of true freedom and fulfillment.

Men Built for Others Profile

Name: Jonathan P. M. Barber
Date of Birth: 5/22/79
Sentence: 15 years-to-life
Parole Eligibility: 7/2018

Leadership Maxim: *Existence is justified by life; life is defined by service.*
Person He Is Most Inspired By: Malcolm X
Favorite Book: *Les Misérables* by Victor Hugo

Education & Interests
- Bachelors of Science in Sociology
- Certified Alcohol and Drug Counselor-Certified Addiction Specialist (CADC-CAS)

Jonathan is a founding member of *Responsibly Driven*, a program that supports DUI offenders (who have been convicted of DUI murder) in becoming accountable for their thinking and the outcomes of their choices. Through his collaboration with Kazu Haga (the founder of the East-Point Peace Academy), Jonathan is also advancing Kingian Nonviolence workshops for prisoners. While maintaining his stance on personal responsibility, and his commitment to live as a Peace Warrior, Jonathan is living his life as a Man Built for Others.

Chapter 10

You must be the change you want to see in the world.

- Mahatma Gandhi

Positive transformation is a powerful experience. It has provided my life with clarity, purpose, and authenticity. Before my rehabilitative process began, I would have quickly offered a sanitized description of my life—including my character shortcomings and past criminality—in the hopes of maintaining a positive self-image. With a radically transformed perspective of personal responsibility, I refuse to be inhibited by the fear of poor opinion. Since embarking on this redemptive journey, I have discovered areas in my life where I have "played the victim" in order to prove myself right. Maintaining such a defensive position only brought cheap moments of selfish happiness while lacking clear vision and true purpose. I hope that my testimonial will illustrate the power of perspective and the importance of humility through an authentic presentation of my life and the ways I distorted reality to justify my irresponsible choices.

I had an ideal childhood. Throughout my younger years, I was blessed with many luxuries and opportunities. Both of my parents were loving and supportive, so there was never a time that I worried about food, clothing, shelter, or abuse. Although we lived in the rough city of Inglewood, California, my parents ensured that I was protected from the neighborhood's dangerous elements through their meticulous selection of schools. My mother adamantly demanded the best education for my brother and me. As a result, my entire childhood education was spent in Catholic schools located outside of Inglewood. You may be wondering, with such a nurturing environment, what happened? So, how did I end up in prison with a life sentence? Well, the meaning that I attached to important childhood events shaped the way that I irresponsibly interacted with the world. In other words, I told myself a dangerous story. Let me explain.

I believe that how we relate to certain life experiences fundamentally constructs a person's perspective of reality. Often, many life experiences may seem trivial to an outsider, but for the individual who lives through such experience(s), triviality can turn into salience. Sometimes, an experience is not isolated. When this occurs, the experience is compounded and takes on a powerfully negative theme. Three such themes have molded my understanding of the world and concept of manhood—loneliness, personal insecurity, and cultural alienation. It took decades for me to recognize the complaints I used to justify my irresponsibility and their significance in my decision-making. Tragically, I was unwilling to consider my erroneous thinking until after I murdered another human being.

Between the ages of four and five, I lived with my mother in Arizona. This was a lonely experience for me because my mom was a flight attendant, which resulted in me often being left with babysitters. I also did not have the luxury of spending time with relatives because the rest of my family lived in either San Diego or Los Angeles—including my father, who resided in Los Angeles for financial reasons. Furthermore, our Arizona residence was in a new track housing development, which contained many vacancies; consequently, children were a rare sighting. I often played in my room alone, and as much as I enjoyed my imaginary world of GI Joe and Justice League of America, I really desired the company of a real friend. It was in Arizona that I developed a serious aversion to loneliness.

Although my father rejoined our household once my mother and I moved back to Inglewood, I was still plagued by loneliness. Since I was a bit older and could ride a bike, I dedicated much of my free time to exploring the neighborhood for kids to play with. Unfortunately, on most days, the neighborhood resembled more of a ghost town than a place to find friends. On those days, I would amuse myself by riding my bike endlessly up and down the streets. Then, there were rare days that I would come across some neighborhood kids, and we would play basketball, football, or Nintendo for hours. Their companionship provided me with most of my happiest memories as a youngster. I continued this quest for companionship throughout my adolescence and into my young adulthood. Avoiding the empty feeling of loneliness became one of the strongest motivators in my life.

In addition to my issues with loneliness, personal insecurities also played a prominent role in my decision-making. During my first year of schooling in California, I believed that I was one of the "cool kids." I did not take school seriously, and I just wanted to have a good time. Then, during the second half of first grade, my eyesight began to severely deteriorate. The deterioration took several weeks, but to a six-year-old, the process seemed instantaneous. I recall talking to a friend when the teacher called for the class's attention. As everyone turned around to face her, I looked up, and the classroom disappeared into a cloudy haze. I stared at the blackboard for what seemed like an eternity as I tried to decipher the blurry scribbles. The teacher eventually noticed that something was wrong and had my friend escort me to the principal's office. The principal's secretary called my parents to inform them that I was having problems with my vision. My father immediately took me to the optometrist who discovered that I had developed a severe astigmatism and needed glasses. For two weeks, I watched the world dance behind a shroud of fog until the optometrist placed a pair of prescription glasses on my head.

Upon arriving at school with my new glasses, kids began to noticeably treat me differently. I was called childish names like "nerd," "geek," and "four-eyes." I didn't understand their reactions or process my experience well. It was just a few weeks prior that I was a "cool kid." Then, all of a sudden, I was being treated as a social outcast. I attributed the alienation to my glasses. Consequently, from that day forward, I decided to become hyper-defensive about any perceived physical defect. This was not my last experience with personal insecurities, but it was certainly one of the most salient events in my life.

The third theme which had a profound effect on my choices was my confusion about my cultural identity. My family is composed of a very diverse ethnic mixture. While we are predominantly African Americans, our skin complexions range from creamy white to onyx black. My father and I are on the lighter side. Growing up in a Black family and neighborhood caused a lot of identity confusion, which created dual realities in my experience. The more I asserted my Blackness, the more the world seemed to resist my efforts. Upon entering high school, this dissonance greatly intensified—since cliques in Los Angeles typically form around ethnicity. My light complexion could pass for various ethnicities, but I immediately noticed the hesitancy that different ethnic groups displayed when I came around. I wasn't Black enough; I wasn't White enough; I didn't speak Spanish. Even two of my closest friends from elementary school distanced themselves from me once we started high school. My uncertainty of group association resurrected past feelings of loneliness and amplified my pre-existing insecurities. I started to compare myself to everyone else, desperately hoping to discover my place in the world. But, no place ever felt quite right. I thought and felt like an outsider and a leper.

Underlying my struggles with loneliness, insecurity, and cultural alienation was a fervent desire for social acceptance. I eventually turned to criminality to satisfy this yearning. On the days that the neighborhood seemed vacant, I chose to associate with the first group of kids I came across. I was still attracted to what I thought were the "cool kids," and that resulted in me ending up in questionable company. While hanging out with these kids, I learned about such crimes as theft and vandalism. Initially, I was reluctant to participate. But over time, my ethical reservations subsided as my desire to be accepted supplanted my concerns about what was "right" and "wrong." All I wanted was to belong with the kids who fit my worldview of fun and excitement.

Over the years, my internal debates of moral behavior continued as my interest in girls developed. During my teenage years, I became extremely interested in female companionship, and I unwisely selected "gangsta" rap as my guide to female courtship. I started listening to "gangsta" rap music in the 5th grade. I found comfort in its smooth harmonies, poetic stories, bold rebellion, and raw authenticity. It was the provocative and taboo nature, however, that appealed to me the most. The "Parental Advisory" sticker on each tape and CD cover screamed out "rebellion," and that message resonated with me. Not only did I feel the need to defy established authorities (i.e., teachers, parents, law enforcement, etc.), but I felt compelled to revolt against past social rejections. I agreed with the "gangsta" rappers' views about how we were oppressed by the world while adopting such beliefs as "F--- the Police," "Down with the Man," and "It's Me Against the World." I adhered to the materialistic and misogynistic concepts of a "man"—pockets full of money, partying 24-7, and other mantras that objectified women. For the next decade, I reacted to the world from this criminal perspective. I whole-heartedly believed that emulating these rappers would make me "cool" and earn me respect.

Being that I was a teen, I began to replace playing games (such as Nintendo and sports) with other activities like smoking and drinking. A friend of mine had a father that allowed us to have small house parties in his basement. I longed for those occasions because it was an opportunity to be around friends—and more specifically, cute girls. I felt like a grown-up who was partaking in the activities that were glorified in the rap songs. I was tired of being an adolescent where social confusion and rejection pervaded my life, so at every opportunity, I rushed to hang out with these friends. Ironically, my friend's father would let us party, but he refused to purchase alcohol for us. So, we had to constantly find different ways to procure alcohol. One of the sad realities of living in Inglewood is the leniency many stores exhibit in the sale of liquor to minors. As I considered this to be an opportunity to prove my "coolness," I would always jump to the task. I cherished the celebration that my peers would unleash upon a successful liquor run. The admiration in the eyes of my friends meant the world to me as it confirmed my distorted thinking.

During these formative years, I began to view parties as the solution to all of my problems. Since rappers constantly boasted about their party lifestyles, and it seemed that parties brought people together, I thought, "Who could be lonely surrounded by crowds of people?" I could. My insecurities would rush to the surface when I got around the party scene. Instead of facing social anxiety with real courage, I sought to escape through the numbing intoxication of alcohol and marijuana. These substances became my artificial courage. I felt that alcohol and drugs relieved my social anxiety; hence, my self-image improved. I would change from a nervous and insecure adolescent to an outgoing, handsome, and exciting adult. With tempered nerves, I presumed that my goals of peer acceptance and admiration were achievable. However, in instances when I experienced social rejection, I found solace in the immature thought, "So what, I'm faded."

Wild and reckless driving was another factor that contributed to my twisted outlook of what "social acceptance" looked like. As a pre-teen, I envisioned a future of freedom, a freedom to go anywhere and do anything that I wanted, a freedom that was dependent on me obtaining my driver's license. In my mind, acquiring a driver's license equated to achieving manhood and a thriving social life. It wasn't "cool" to be driven around by one's parents. Rappers drove flashy cars with booming stereo systems while women swooned over them. Therefore, for all the wrong reasons, I decided that it was of critical importance that I got a license and a car.

I used the distance between my house, my high school, and my friends (which was a one-way distance of 20-miles) to justify my distorted beliefs about the purpose of driving. I had no problem riding a bike around Inglewood, but scurrying back and forth across Los Angeles County was impossible without a car. When I finally received my driver's license and bought a car, I was able to travel across Los Angles to visit my friends. I was able to participate in high school sports, go out on dates, and experience other activities that I feared I would miss. My sense of personal value had been reduced to owning a car, which I viewed as necessary to maintain my social life and self-image.

It was my fear of "missing out on something" that prompted the deadly habit of driving dangerously. I convinced myself that in order to stay relevant in the party scene, I had to be at every social function. If there were multiple parties in one night, I would rush from one side of Los Angeles County to the other. To a certain extent, it was a race between me and loneliness, a race where I refused to slow down or pay attention to the stop signs. I drove extremely fast, took numerous shortcuts, and disregarded most traffic laws. I needed to make an appearance everywhere to ensure that people did not forget about me or leave me behind. Like many naïve young men, I considered myself to be an excellent driver with superior skills. I felt that law-abiding citizens were actually clogging up my streets, which I thought entitled me to drive fast and recklessly.

In my mind, what was wrong and illegal for others did not apply to me. I believed that I was above the law. This criminal way of thinking is how I justified my decision to drive under the influence (DUI). Anytime the opportunity presented itself, I would get high on marijuana. I told myself ridiculous stories that marijuana should be legal because it is all natural; therefore, I felt I was entitled to use it. In addition, my glorification of the rap culture offered plenty of other justifications. I would tell my self, "This is what we do, smoke weed and get high." I fed the distorted belief that marijuana did not inhibit any of my motor skills, so after becoming stoned, I would drive without regard for the consequences. Since I believed using drugs and alcohol "enhanced" my social life, it was inevitable that I stayed high. Many times, I would even "hot-box" my car (let it fill up with marijuana smoke) as I drove around town. Just like the rap videos, I ignorantly believed it was cool showing up to a place with marijuana smoke creeping out as I exited the car.

After I graduated from high school, and began attending San Diego State University (SDSU), I expanded my substance abuse to more serious mind-altering drugs. Although I lived on campus and did not drive often, my mindset to engage in dangerous activities while intoxicated remained. The story

I told myself was that the "college experience" necessitated that I adopt a hardcore party lifestyle of womanizing and getting wasted. Similar to when I was in high school, my desire to be accepted surfaced. Thus, I reverted to what I believed had worked for me in the past—drinking alcohol and smoking marijuana. I took the party lifestyle even further in college because I believed that the harder I partied, the more social admiration I would gain.

My decisions continued to worsen as time went on, specifically my decision to drive while intoxicated. At this point in my life, I had attached more significance to having a car so I could get from place to place. My social network ranged from San Diego all the way to Santa Barbara, so my social relations rested on my ability to travel (at least this is what I told myself). With more parties to attend, I began driving while intoxicated on an array of illicit substances. By this time, the decision to behave in such a dangerous and careless manner was not difficult with the mindset that I had created. Since I had been driving under the influence of marijuana for years, the transition to drive while under the influence of alcohol and/or some other drug was seamless. Not only did I completely disregard the consequences of my choices, but I became callous towards the welfare of others. My false sense of invincibility convinced me that the concept of safety did not apply to me. Driving while intoxicated may be dangerous for others, but not for me. The story I told myself was, "I have driven home on hallucinogenic drugs while King Kong chased me down the freeway and dolphins flew over my head. I am an excellent intoxicated driver. I would never be a character in one of those countless, tragic DUI stories. I am special." As long as I was coherent enough to make my key turn the ignition switch, I was fully capable of operating a motor vehicle.

Back in 2000, I received a 30-day sojourn in the Santa Barbara County Jail (SBCJ). Since I was considered a "first-timer" and classified as a nonviolent offender (convicted of drug possession and sales of psilocybin mushrooms), I was sent to the "Honor Dorm." Then, seeing as how I was provided with numerous amenities such as weights, cigarettes, and a pool table, I believed "doing time" was easy. I left SBCJ with an inflated ego and a sense of invincibility. The threat of incarceration no longer scared me. In addition, my probation was being supervised by Orange County, so my probation officer could not arrest me without permission. I was convinced that Santa Barbara would not violate my probation, so for the next three years, I operated with the criminal mentality of "catch me if you can."

In 2003, while driving under the influence, I murdered an innocent lady as she and her husband were riding their motorcycles home from a date together. After the collision, my car burst into flames, and I fled into the blackness of the night. The only thing I cared about was my selfish desire to get away. I did not want to be held accountable for my choices that led to this horrific outcome. Eventually, I was arrested, tried, convicted, and sentenced to 15 years-to-life for second-degree murder and gross vehicular manslaughter.

I wish I could write that my victim's death was the catalyst for my transformation, and since then, I have been the exemplar of rehabilitation. Unfortunately, that is simply not the case. Often, I think about all of the experiences I denied her and her family. While I did commit my life to sobriety that night, sobriety was not the only demon I was battling. For years, I constructed a distorted and irresponsible perspective of reality, one that was rooted in personal fears, unresolved childhood experiences, and antisocial coping mechanisms. I was running hard and fast to stay in front of loneliness and to avoid confronting my insecurities. Responsibility required too much effort. It was easier (and more fun) to live wildly. The sad truth is that it took the death of an innocent woman and a life-sentence to instigate honest introspection in my life. Through this journey of introspection, there have been great leaps of discovery, but there have also been a few discouraging obstructions and regressions. The obstacle that brought my cycle of denial to an abrupt halt was *prison politics*.

As a kid, I relished the rebellious thought of being an outlaw. However, once I entered Orange County Jail (OCJ) and was confronted with *prison politics*, I realized that I was utterly oblivious to the realities of the prison culture and in denial of the consequences of my irresponsibility. Unlike SBCJ, OCJ is governed by inmate-imposed mores called *prison politics*. Established under the pretense of safety, prisoners in the California Department of Corrections and Rehabilitation (CDCR) have and enforced these mores over the course of several decades. Ethnicity plays a fundamental role in this process, but gang affiliation is the ultimate arbiter.

When a new person arrives in a housing sector, inmates assess the person's affiliation. Generally, this is easily done since affiliation is ethnic-based. In instances of uncertainty, a person is asked, "Who do you run with?" This question identifies whose side they're on. For first-timers who aren't gang affiliated, this assessment can come as a surprise, especially for those who hold themselves above racism. For a multiethnic person like myself, this confrontation can be quite complex, especially when my White and Black heritages are opposing factions in prison. What side do you take?

Then there are little nuances that arise in certain cases, such as when one group refuses to allow a person to "roll with" (select) their adversary. The logic behind this stance is that the person is viewed as being "disloyal." This can transpire even when there is only a perceived affiliation, meaning the debated person only looks like they belong to their group. These sorts of disputes can lead to a lot of violence. I encountered this exact situation due to my ambiguous ethnic appearance.

The night that I was processed into the OCJ, I was dreadfully intoxicated. As I entered the inmate-housing unit, I was asked, "Who do you run with—Wood, Southern, Paisa, Asian, or Black?" I replied in a drunk mumble, "Black." Noticing that I was utterly inebriated, the inmates resignedly pointed me to a bunk and left me alone. After several days of learning about the mores of *prison politics*, I came to realize that my declaration was incorrect and subsequently decided to "roll with" the *Others*. *Others* are composed of Asians, Native Americans, South Americans, and other miscellaneous groups.

Switching allegiance is a very controversial and sensitive matter in prison. The fact that I was heavily inebriated upon entering, uninformed about *prison politics*, and a first-timer (I had never been to prison) helped to quickly correct the issue. Although both groups were amenable to the solution, I never resolved this internal conflict. All of the internal themes that plagued me during my adolescence and young adulthood resurfaced. The dissonance from picking sides created feelings of ethnic alienation. Consequently, I started to question my cultural identification again. I thought such things as, "Why do I have to choose sides?" "Will they accept me?" "Do I need to prove my ethnicity?" Plus, as I was now isolated from my friends and family, feelings of loneliness haunted me constantly. I thought, "Once again, I'm all alone." In addition to my personal insecurities of peer acceptance, I became exceedingly concerned with my physical safety.

The way I mitigated my negative feelings of "fitting in" was by becoming another cog in the wheel of *prison politics*. "Fitting in" entails conforming to the mores of *prison politics*. For those aligned with the *Others,* the majority of those rules and norms do not require a continuance of irresponsible and criminal behavior, but they do require a person not to make waves for the group. I accomplished this by not taking on debts or getting into fights, especially with other factions.

Simply "fitting in" was not sufficient to quiet my inner doubts. Just as when I engaged in my adolescent liquor runs, I eagerly inserted myself into group conflicts that otherwise could have possibly been avoided. I convinced myself that the way to gain acceptance and admiration was by showing the *Others* that I was willing support their "cause." On higher security level prison yards, these opportunities usually arise during group confrontations, which require inmates to participate in riots.

Any Rules Violation Report (RVR) puts a life-term inmate's parole in serious jeopardy. An RVR for "participation in a riot" carries significant weight in the parole commissioners' consideration and will most likely result in a denial of parole.

All of these factors came to mind on one particular day when I was playing in the yard with three friends. In the middle of the game, there was an eerie quietness that forewarned of imminent danger. One of my friends noticed that the *Others* were being attacked by the baseball diamond on the other side of the yard. Instantly, my two friends turned and ran towards the chaos. In what seemed to be an automatic response, I sprinted after them. During that dash, I thought about the reoccurring themes in my life (loneliness, personal insecurities, and cultural alienation). I also thought about my victim and her family. Then there was my family, my role in *prison politics*, and my parole eligibility. My inner conversation felt like it was endless as I tossed arguments back and forth in my mind. My head was racing with thoughts such as, "There goes your parole date." "If you don't get down, you'll lose respect." "I bet this is over something stupid." "I can't believe these idiots got me into this mess." "Would they come to your defense?" "You'll have to watch your back forever if you don't participate." And, "Here's your moment to shine." By the time I arrived at the melee, I made the decision to observe the rules of *prison politics,* and I deemed them to be more important than my other commitments. Hence, I threw myself into the fray.

I made similar poor decisions throughout the first few years of my incarceration. It was not until I finally got tired of being a hypocrite that I started taking genuine steps towards my transformation. I cannot recall the actual day or instance. It occurred over the course of a series of events. One thing is for sure, I grew tired of compromising my values for the superficial, short-term payoffs of my continued criminality. An extra tray of food was not worth my integrity. The luxuries of unrestricted phone calls and internet access that were afforded by possessing an illegal cell phone were not worth my possible freedom someday. Wanting to be right, popular, and "cool" wasn't worth the lost opportunities with my family and true friends who had my best interests at heart. The tradeoff between the consequences of instant gratification and the future I wanted to have simply became too apparent. I made the decision to directly address my character shortcomings and to begin making amends for the irreparable harm that I caused. In order to accomplish this task, I needed to rediscover the values that my parents instilled in me. I needed to clearly identify the people and things in my life that are most important. I needed to create a future vision and embrace its impending challenges.

My road to transformation is marked with moments of insight, the development of prosocial tools, attitude adjustments, and paradigms shifts; yet, there were three events that radically impacted the way I responded to life. The first event came while I was training to become a state-certified Alcohol and Other Drugs (AOD) counselor. It was during this experience that I became aware of my temptation to objectify people. The second revelation came from my involvement with Rabbi Yochanan Friedman who helped me clarify my life purpose, which is to be of service. The third event that profoundly influenced my transformation came from my membership in the Cemanahuac Cultural Group (CCG), which provided an environment for me to become reacquainted with humanity and to learn to appreciate our common values and interrelatedness.

Knowing that I have a long history of substance abuse, it was a wise decision to discover responsible ways to uncover my underlying issues in order to prevent future relapses. In 2011, Eugene Dey and several other friends encouraged me to enroll in Palo Verde College's Alcohol and Drugs Studies (ADS) program. Upon his release, Eugene teamed up with the Crop Organization to certify a collection of ADS graduates. In order to qualify for state certification, applicants were required to accrue a certain number of supervised training hours. Eugene adopted the *Leadership-4-Life* (L4L) program (a transformational "way of being" program) to satisfy this requirement. During the video training portion of this program, I was given the opportunity to see myself on video. This was when I became aware of the ways I showed up when I stopped caring about people. It wasn't pretty.

Humans must justify their decisions to cause harm. The justifications can range from disgustingly petty to morally imperative. Whatever the case, an excuse is formed. My preferred justification was the objectification of my fellow human beings. By objectifying people, I could deny all of the courtesies a person deserves—respect, love, empathy, patience, etc.—without feeling guilt or remorse. When I viewed women as mere trophies, other drivers and pedestrians as things in my way, drug users as quick paydays, or friends as nothing more than sources of entertainment, I stripped away their humanity. The temptation to objectify people was alluring to me because it distanced me from responsibility. I could take everything I wanted from a person without any personal attachment or accountability for how my actions affected them. I have come to understand that those were the short-term payoffs. Sadly, I also learned that the long-term costs of objectification are incredibly destructive and full of pain.

As a small child, I yearned for a friend. My behavior throughout high school and college revealed the desperate lengths that I would go to in order to gain social acceptance. But, I was not seeking true companionship. All of my relationships were nothing more than fleeting encounters of superficiality. I lost valuable opportunities to nurture and appreciate the relationships I had with my family. Although my younger brother and I grew up in the same house, we are sadly more strangers than brothers because of my objectifying ways. My half-sisters and their children barely know who I am. I have lost multiple family elders without having the chance to say "goodbye." I am an outsider to the new generation of my family. My social relationships reflected the same superficial nature. I can hardly recall the names of the girls who I slept with; and the people who were closest to me have moved on with their lives.

I objectified these people by making them "things" to be tolerated until my satisfaction was attained. After years of reflection, I finally admitted that I was only fooling myself. I constructed emotional barriers to serve my insecurities, which essentially perpetuated my loneliness and proved the insecurities right. It is a daily battle with my temptation to objectify, but I am determined to resist it.

A couple of years ago, two friends of mine (named Eric and Don) invited me to assist Rabbi Friedman, the Correctional Training Facility's Jewish Chaplain, in creating a self-help group based on his father's "life and existence" paradigm. This perspective is grounded in humility, and it essentially defines an individual's existence as utterly unnecessary for the functionality of the universe—since the universe will continue perfectly with or without that person. A person justifies his/her "existence" by celebrating "life," and by this I mean finding ways to enhance the lives of others. The purpose of humanity is to be of service, to be needed. For the majority of my life, I have done the complete opposite by increasing the burden of others. I have demanded emotional, financial, and physical support from the very people who genuinely care for me while having minimal regards for their well-being. I was a human leech. When I am at my best, I approach my relationships from an "other-preservation" perspective, as opposed to my old mindset of "self-preservation." When I am at my best, I am celebrating "life" by identifying and acting on those moments where I can lessen the burden of someone's existence. One of the most powerful lessons that I learned during my incarceration is that "life is not about me."

My involvement with Cemanahuac Cultural Group (CCG) helped me discover my humanity through its promotion of multiculturalism and social justice through nonviolent means. This environment has been perfect for me to explore the concept of "culture" and its roles in my life. For years, I entertained a limited understanding of "culture," believing that it was strictly an ethnically based concept. What I found, however, is that shared beliefs and customs form the nucleus of a particular "culture," not the ethnic composition of the group. My commitment to CCG has taught me that the majority of cultures are founded on a similar set of core values, and this commonality reveals our humanity. Although our world is beautifully diverse, we all desire similar things—security, prosperity, family, and freedom. My criminality stunted the realization of my humanity while denying others the opportunity to express their humanity in a full and meaningful way. My life's purpose today is to empower and strengthen others' humanity. I do this through my promotion of *Kingian Nonviolence Conflict Reconciliation (KNCR)* and advocacy for social justice. *KNCR* training has taught me that social justice can only be achieved by looking deeper than cultural stereotypes and generalizations. I have come to believe that through the practical application of *KNCR* and multiculturalism, each person's humanity is revealed. Today, I am committed to honoring humanity.

I am a man with many flaws and I am okay admitting that. In my criminal years, I utilized all sorts of mechanisms and ploys to cover them up. So many hours of my day were wasted on this self-involvement process. It was a wickedly torturous ride to nowhere. Tired, I needed to get off. In doing so, I came across many opportunities. My transformational journey has many more miles ahead, but my map is clearly charted. I am committed to living a life for others because the essence of humanity is our interrelatedness and that should be revered.

In the book *Act Like a Success, Think Like a Success*, Steve Harvey identifies the dash on a person's tombstone as the most important aspect. The dash symbolizes the deceased person's life; it represents the accomplishments he/she achieved and the relationships he/she fostered. Accomplishing personal aspirations is fantastic, but this does not establish your legacy. A legacy is composed of all of the time, energy, and love you invested in other human beings. When Steve shared this anecdote, he wanted the reader to understand that regardless of your strengths or weaknesses, there are always ways to bring value to another's life. Do not be distracted by trivialities—life is too short. When someone reminisces about your funeral, what will the dash on your tombstone mean to him or her?

Men Built for Others Profile

Name: Gilbert Rosales
Date of Birth: 1/6/72
Sentence: 30 years-to-life
Parole Eligibility: 7/2018

Leadership Maxim: *Why pay someone when you can do it yourself?*
Person He Is Most Inspired By: His older brother, Eric Rosales
Favorite Book: *Humble Pie*

Education & Interests
- Certificate of Completion in Business
- Associate of Science (in progress)

Gilbert is a man who understands that leadership has nothing to do with titles. He is a consummate team player who is willing to lead by example from any position. For anyone willing to look, Gilbert is an example of what it looks like to shift priorities and begin living into a future worth having. He is a committed friend, a loving husband, and is living his life as a Man Built for Others.

Chapter 11

*The depth of your struggle will
determine the height of your success.*

\- R. Kelly

I was born in 1972 and came to prison at the age of eighteen for the senseless killing of another Hispanic male. I do not know when I will be released, but I know that the pain and loss I have caused others will not be erased regardless of where I am. Although I cannot undo the harm I have caused, through a series of turning points, I have become committed to a responsible lifestyle of caring for the welfare of others. I have also learned to look for ways to use my past as an instrument for positive development in myself and others.

On a Friday night in October of 1990, I shot and killed a young man for disrespecting a teenage girl. At the time, I actually felt heroic for having committed a murder. With the belief system that I had built, I saw myself as a knight in shining armor rather than as the street hoodlum I actually was.

I began to develop this bizarre belief as a child. After my mother left (when I was six-months-old), my father raised me and my two siblings. My father was good to us in many ways, and because I was the youngest, he sometimes showed me special favor. He often took me trucking in his rig, stopping at different places and letting me buy trinkets and other keepsakes (which I still have). He showed me how to work with my hands and fix things, saying to me, "Why pay someone else when you can do it yourself?" I have warm memories of sitting in the living room with my dad, brother, and sister watching television shows like Hogan's Heroes and Johnny Carson. And every Friday he took us to a pizza place where I still remember the smell, sounds, and closeness that I felt with my family. To this day, whenever there is a pizza sale at the prison, I buy one because of the memories it stirs. To summarize how I felt about my dad, one day when I was eleven, I said to him, "If you died, I would want to die."

With all of the goodness that my dad showed us, there was one problem that was present in our home. When he drank, he could be verbally and physically abusive, often exploding unpredictably with violent attacks—sometimes with his fists and other times with whatever instrument he could grab at the moment. His violence, which showed up any time he was drinking and females were present (especially my sister), overshadowed my life while I was growing up. When I watched or listened to my sister scream and cry as my father beat her, I would imagine myself taking action to protect her. Then, one day when I was thirteen, I did. That incident was a turning point in how I saw myself.

On that day, I was in our living room when I heard my father yelling at my sister in her bedroom. It was about something she had done at school. The yelling went on for a while, and then I heard her scream when he began to hit her. As usual, I wanted to help, but I was afraid. It went on and on, my father yelling and my sister screaming. Finally, I said to myself, "I'm letting her down." I felt like a coward for just sitting there. I jumped up and ran into her bedroom. She was sitting on the edge of her bed and my father was standing over her, hitting her with his hands. I ran across the room and put my arms around my sister to shield her. My father then started hitting me. At first, I was passively taking the blows and hoping he would stop. But he continued, until I yelled, "Enough!" I stood up, faced him, and then slugged him in the stomach. When I did this, he stopped. His eyes and facial expression showed that he was surprised. He stood still for a couple of seconds, and then he turned and walked out of the room.

My father never hit any of us again. I felt very proud of myself, very manly and in control, like I was a lady's hero. The wrong lesson that I learned is that "violence works." I had brought safety to our home, and I was a protector of the helpless. These are the ideas about myself that I began using to build my self-image, not just in the home, but everywhere.

As a child, I struggled with schoolwork, and I did not learn to read until I was twenty-six. At age nine, my school placed me in the Special Education class, and I felt humiliated by this. By that time, I had already internalized the idea that I was "stupid" (that is how I thought of myself). But I had become very skilled in figuring out ways to keep people from seeing my weakness. For example, when I knew I would have a reading assignment, I would spend hours memorizing (as best I could) the paragraph. By doing this, I was able to make everyone think I was reading, when in fact, I was basically reciting what I had spent hours memorizing. That was just one of the ways I kept others from noticing my deep belief that I was dumb and inferior. During those years, I learned to focus on my actions and avoid my feelings. I was a boy with a mask, afraid to let my weaknesses (real or imagined) be exposed. I was driven to do whatever seemed necessary in order to disguise what I believed was weakness or inferiority. This way of thinking was a major factor in many of my decisions, including killing a person who posed no actual threats to me.

The day that I committed murder, a group of guys embarrassed me in front of some girls. After leaving the scene of embarrassment, I remember how my friends and I felt humiliated. By this time in my life, I had conditioned myself to think that the only way to respond to this experience was with violence.

I called a friend who I knew had a gun and asked him to let me use it. After he gave me the gun, we returned to the place from which we fled. My only conscious thought was that I wanted to show everyone I was strong, willing to stick up for the girls, and that I was not scared (even though I was). When we arrived and the violence broke out, we again decided to flee. We piled into our car and began to leave. A man in the middle of the street began running toward us. From the inside of our car, I aimed the gun and fired. I saw him fall to the ground.

I was arrested just thirty minutes later. When I was told that I had killed a man and that I was going to be charged with murder, I did not feel much about it either way. I thought at the time I did the right thing. I felt no remorse for my victim. I had little concern about going to prison.

Since childhood, I had learned to focus on what I needed to do—what actions I needed to take in order to survive and show myself as being strong. As was normal for me then, I gave little attention to how I felt about any of it. One man was dead, his family was devastated, my own family was suffering, and I was going to prison for a very long time. But to me, all of those things were just facts to deal with. I did not allow myself to experience or pay attention to what I felt. This is how I lived and survived. But one day, something started to change. Although the process took years, it was the testimony of the sister of the man I had killed that started my transformation.

On the witness stand, as the family members of the man I murdered were given the opportunity to speak, the father expressed hatred toward me. He made angry statements like, "He should die in prison." But when the victim's sister got on the stand, she talked about her pain but also demonstrated compassion. She said to the court, "I don't know why Mr. Rosales killed my brother. I don't want him to go to prison for the rest of his life. But, I want him to be there long enough to understand what he did and how it has affected me and my family."

When she said this, my arrogance caused me to resist her words. But years later, the memory of her voice and facial expressions played a strong role in my transformation. Although I did not realize it at the time, she had shown me a way of looking at life that was different than my own experience and conditioning.

After being sentenced to 25 years-to-life, my attitude was, "Okay, I'm a teenager with a life sentence. Well, that's just how it is, and I'll keep moving forward." I started my long journey through the prison system, focusing on what I needed to do in order to blend in. I got tattoos, learned the lingo, learned the rules, and played the game the way I was expected to in the prison culture. I asked my long-term girlfriend, Bernadette, to marry me, and she agreed. Because she knew the length of my sentence, I believe she had reservations about the marriage but felt obligated to me. At that time, I did not care enough to ask about such things. I wanted a wife, and I regulated my life by what I wanted rather than by how my words and actions affected others.

In the prison, from day-to-day, I participated in activities like playing handball and learning how to draw. These things enabled me to totally focus on what I was doing in the moment and to forget everything else for hours at a time. I had no long-term goals or any sense of a larger meaning of life. I focused on enjoying what I could and totally putting my interests into what I was doing on that day.

Two years after my arrest, my sister and wife visited me. As soon as we sat down at the table, my sister said, "We have some news." I stared at her face, knowing from her tone and expression that whatever was coming next would not be nice to hear. She said, "Dad was killed." I felt numb. We all sat in silence as they stared at me with an expression like, "What is he going to do?" I struggled to process how my world had changed by what I had just heard. Dad is no longer living. My life is no longer the same. It seemed that so much was left unfinished, and all of this was something I could not regard as just a "fact."

Finally, I spoke and asked for details. My sister cautiously described how our dad had a dispute with his landlord and how it ended with the other man senselessly killing our father. As she talked, I filled my mind with rage (along with the grief). The rest of the visit was subdued. We tried some light talk, but nothing really worked. When I left the visiting room and returned to my cell, it seemed that everything was different.

In my dad's disappointment, he had distanced himself from me after my arrest, and our contact had been limited. In my cell, I pulled out an envelope with a letter he had written me. I stared at his handwriting and his name on the return address. I told myself, "When this guy who killed my dad comes to prison, I'll get transferred to wherever he is, and I'll get the payback." I held that attitude for years.

Life went on. Although I learned to push down the grief and anger about my dad, it was there. Then, when I was twenty-four, my wife asked for a divorce. I saw it coming. She was visiting less, writing less, and expressing less of herself to me. During those years, I had become more cold, arrogant, and emotionally detached. This, together with the length of my sentence, pushed my wife further and further away until she turned to someone else.

When Bernadette left, I said to myself, "I'm not going to be weak. I won't let myself lose sleep over it." That was my old, tried, and proven strategy for dealing with the hard issues of life: "Just don't deal with it at all." Accept facts; ignore feelings, and focus on what I can enjoy in the moment. My view of life did not extend beyond that. And although I was not "happy," I was comfortable in my tiny mental prison.

I was able to stay out of serious trouble in prison, and in 2000 (at the age of twenty-nine), I was transferred to a lower level facility in Soledad (CTF-Central).

The first thing I noticed at CTF was the older population and the laidback attitude of the inmates. In prison, there is a political structure organized around race and affiliation. In the harder prisons, such as the ones I had been serving time in for about ten years, the structure is tight. Any violations are answered with discipline—sometimes with execution. But in Soledad, the structure was loose and not strongly enforced. I could play handball and other sports with inmates of different races, and I felt good about this. In prison, for the sake of personal safety and acceptance with my group, I went along with the policy of strict, racial separation (even though within myself I did not feel prejudice). So at CTF, I began to loosen up, let down my guard, and gradually became open to new ways of thinking about myself and about life in general.

In 2007, I began attending what are called "self-help" groups. I knew a lot of inmates who were doing this, and now that I had reached my mid-thirties, I was thinking that the groups might by a way for me to experience new things. I did not know what to expect from the groups. And for the first couple of years, I basically attended them without giving serious thought to how I could benefit (or even thinking that I needed to benefit). What helped me gain a sense of clarity was a statement by a Board of Parole Hearing (BPH) commissioner at my 2009 parole hearing.

At that hearing, I was denied parole for five years. Near the end, the commissioner said to me, "You're an enigma to us." In the days and months after the hearing, those words bounced around inside of me. I started thinking, "I'm getting close to forty. I've been in prison since I was a teenager. I don't want to grow old and die in prison. What do I need to do to get out of here? What can I do to get back to my family?"

For many years, I hadn't thought much about getting out of prison. For about a twenty-year period, hardly any lifers were paroled in California. But in the mid-2000s, a shift occurred, and the BPH began finding lifers "suitable for parole." This gave me new hope. So, after I received the five-year denial, I committed myself to putting in the hard work required for a favorable decision from the parole authorities. This meant I would need to vastly improve my insight into why I had become a person who could so callously kill another. So in 2010, although it was for selfish reasons (wanting to get out of prison), I made a choice to participate in the groups with the goal of developing self-insight and whatever else could help me show the BPH that I was no longer a risk to public safety. But one thing I remained unwilling to do was give up using illegal cell phones. I justified it by saying, "It's the only thing that keeps my family close to me." At that time, the person I was most concerned about in the family was my grandmother.

My grandma had been ill for years with general health issues, and I knew the day of her leaving us was coming. We talked often, and it hurt to think of her alone in her house with only memories of happier times. She had been good to me all of my life, and I loved her very much. My mom and one of my aunts visited her daily to look after her, but my grandma deserved for me to be there, and I was not. One day, my sister sent me a text on my cell phone: "Grandma is in the hospital and she's not doing well." I was able to call her at the hospital. She could barely talk, but I knew she was listening. After the call, I accepted that her time on earth was coming to an end. I consoled myself by knowing that she was a woman with strong faith in Christ, and she would soon be with Grandpa. But still, I felt something so precious being ripped away from me. A few days later, my sister sent a message: "Grandma is gone." That was in April of 2011.

Although I had never been close with my mom, during the same year that my grandma died, I learned that my mom had cancer. "It's in my lungs," she said. At the prison where I was housed, I worked in the medical department. So I asked the medical staff questions, and I was told that it looks bad. I started calling my mom a lot, and realized I loved her more than I realized. One day, I asked her, "Why did you leave Dad?" She said what I already suspected, that she was terrified of my dad. I asked her why she did not make more of an effort to be close to us. She told me, "Mijo, you don't know how much I wanted to, but after I left, your father warned me that they would find my body buried in Mexico if I didn't stay away."

One day, I got a text from my sister, the same as when Grandma was sick. "Mom isn't doing well. I think you need to talk to her." I called Mom for the last time. And at the end of our talk, she said in a very tender voice, "I love you, Mijo." A few days later, my sister told me, "Mom is gone." My mother's beautiful last words stayed in my ears. But it seemed like everything was piling up, the special people in my world leaving me one by one. When I was starting my prison sentence as a teenager, I had not paused to think that it would someday come to this. That night on my bunk, I cried like a baby.

I turned my focus to the groups and began preparing for my next hearing in 2014. I was doing well in most areas, but

I still kept the phone. I called my remaining family members often, and I reconnected with my best friend (Marcela), whom I had known since we were twelve. After a couple months of phone contact, Marcela visited, and things picked up between us. She came every month, and one day she told me, "Gilbert, I have loved you since I was a kid, and I will always love you. I'm here for you, but you will have to ask me to be your wife." I still had a few years until my next hearing, and I felt concern about starting a marriage with so much unknown hanging over us. One day while she was visiting me, I laid everything out—what I'm facing, the uncertainty of when I'll be released, and how I cannot physically be there when she is feeling alone and without companionship. Of course, she already knew all of this, but I wanted to put it all in front of us. She listened and nodded. Then she squeezed my hand, and while staring into my eyes, she assured me that she had already thought about this. When she told me that, I felt at peace. On our next visit, I proposed. It was a beautiful moment—holding her hand, looking into her eyes, and watching her light up with anticipation. We set our wedding date for July 13, 2013. We were excited, and it seemed that so much in my life was coming together.

In June of that year, two weeks before the wedding (and nine months before my hearing), I was caught with the cell phone.

At the hearing, the panel denied me parole for three more years, specifically for the phone. Although I had decided to make some changes to move away from criminal thinking, my choice to not go all the way (to hold back and leave myself the option of bending the rules where I felt I could justify it), came with a heavy price.

In the past, I would have shrugged this off or cast blame. But after my parole denial, I took to heart my failures and my responsibility for them, and that's when I turned to God for help. I said a prayer that went something like, "I know You are always watching. Keep me aware of You. Bless me to use these three years to truly grow and be ready for my next hearing."

From that point, it seemed that everything—the loss of family members, Marcella's disappointment, my advancing age, the parole denial—it was all working together to change how I felt about myself and my responsibility to God and to others. I noticed a fresh motivation, and I did not want to lose it.

I went all in with the groups. I viewed it as a challenge because I had never seen myself as a person who could talk in front of others and keep them interested. I started putting myself out there. I took a job as a captain's porter in an area where there were always officers and authorities (whom we call "higher-ups.") I looked for opportunities to start conversations with them. Nobody else knew it, but I was experiencing something very new. I realized that I could talk with staff members effectively, not only about serious things, but even casually and with humor. Between speaking up in groups and talking at my job, I noticed my confidence building. Then, in one of the groups, I was offered the opportunity to be videotaped while talking to my peers.

When I first heard the offer about the video, I felt a knot in my stomach—like a heavy hand was pressing on my chest. But I acknowledged the old pattern of shying away from challenges and I dismissed it. We did the video, and I talked about my childhood belief of being a protector of women and how this connected to my crime. As I spoke, I was surprised by how well I was doing. I did not choke, lose my focus, or ramble. Afterward, we all sat down to watch the video. I looked up at the screen and suddenly saw my face. For the first time in my life, I was watching and listening to myself.

I saw that I looked arrogant in my facial expression and body posture. But, as I continued talking, I also noticed that what I was saying made sense. I felt amazed at how clearly I was telling my story and connecting my life experiences. I realized that it is easy as long as I'm just telling the truth and saying what I really believe. I smiled and rubbed my hands as I saw how my new practice of speaking up (even when I felt intimidated) was paying off. I did not like the arrogance, but I told myself, "I'm going to correct that." The arrogance was a look that I cultivated as a child when I did not want anyone to know how humiliated I felt after I was put in the Special Education class. It was my life-long mask, and now it was time to take it off.

After this, I deliberately began involving myself with other people outside of my normal group on a more regular basis. I started to understand that what they have to say is just as important as what I have to say, and I could find value in their way of seeing the world. I signed up for more groups, such as the Gavel Club, which would help me overcome my fear of speaking (and even reading) in front of others. In the groups, and in conversations outside of the groups, I focused on gaining a much deeper insight into the factors that led me to commit murder, as well as other areas of self-insight that are truly necessary to be found suitable for parole. I was learning to look at myself and at life from a different perspective, to not be locked into just one point of view. And I was learning that it's okay to accept feelings, that life is more than just "facts."

I began to facilitate groups, including anger management. It was then, for the first time in my life, I learned to stop and think about what anger even is and why it had been such a major force in my life since childhood. I felt empowered by all of this—sharing my experiences, telling my story, getting feedback from others, and giving feedback to them. But the biggest turning point of all came from listening to a female who was a victim of a violent crime.

I was attending a group in which crime victims came into the prison and told their stories. One woman described how her family had suffered terribly during a home invasion in which her husband was murdered. She explained how this shattered her world and left her living each day in fear, rage, and bitterness. But after some time, she realized what those feeling would do to her if she held on to them. She decided that she wanted to be free from her pain, and one of the ways she did this was by becoming an advocate for the release of the men who had victimized her. As I watched her face and listened to her words, I thought about my trial and the courtroom testimony of the sister of the man I murdered. I felt something shift in my mind—it was a new awareness of how I had caused another family to suffer. After I left the group that day, this awareness stayed with me.

I didn't talk to anyone about this—not for a while. It seemed I was entering a part of the world that I had closed myself off to for most of my life. I was letting myself feel what others feel and letting myself experience what I feel. I thought about the man who killed my dad, and I felt like a hypocrite for holding against another person what I myself had done to someone else. This kept coming back to me. Then, one day when I was alone in my cell, I made the decision to forgive this man (a person whom I did not know, but hated for so long). When I forgave him, I experienced more than just a feeling of release. I felt like something about me changed, like who and what kind of person I was had shifted.

I called my brother. He had also expressed a lot of rage toward the man who killed our father. I said to him, "There's no need for us to continue holding on to the hatred. If we hold on to it, we'll stay in that darkness." My brother stayed quiet for a moment, and then said, "I get it." We never spoke about it again.

I started talking about this experience. And whether those conversations took place in or outside of a self-help group, I noticed that people were showing me a different kind of respect. It was different than the old respect. I could see that others were experiencing me in a new way. They were coming to me and wanting to talk about serious things in their lives, or they were asking me to step into leadership roles in other groups. I felt comfortable with this, like I was becoming the real me and leaving behind the role that I used to play.

But I had still been shying away from the biggest challenge of all. When I was 18, I killed a man, and I told myself that he had it coming. I would say to myself, "He would have had no problem shooting me, so why should I feel bad about shooting him?" For many years, that way of thinking had worked for me. But now, it was nagging at me, like some unfinished business that could no longer be ignored. I started letting myself think more about him, remembering what I knew about him. He was not just a fact. He was a human being with memories, plans, and people he loved. He had two young children whom I caused to grow up with only memories of their father. I took away the opportunity for him to watch his children grow, to stand at their weddings, and to hold his grandchildren. I can only imagine his children's experience on the day they were told that their father was gone. Not to mention the experience of many others whose world I changed in a painful way.

I started sharing this experience with some of my friends and in the groups that I attended. The more I talked about it, the more it came alive to me. It was like something I had buried down in a basement, and now it was all coming up. I had senselessly killed a person who was a father, a son, a brother, and a friend. His family woke up that morning having no idea they would never see him again. They would not have a chance to say goodbye, to give him one last hug, or to get closure on any unresolved issues. I left them with that pain.

One night, while I was lying on my bunk, I stopped resisting. I told myself, "Just let it happen." I used my imagination, and it was like watching it all in a movie. I saw the father of my victim getting the phone call, gripping the receiver, and his face tightening with grief as he tried to think how he could bring this news to the rest of his family—to the mother of his dead son and to the sister who would later plant her words in my soul from a witness stand. It was then that I knew I was breaking free from a prison I had lived in since childhood. I was experiencing what the suffering woman in the courtroom meant when she said that she wanted me to understand.

Afterword

"Greater love has no one than this, than to lay down one's life for his friends."

John 15:33, New King James Version

In the fall of 2016, Jason, Rich, Matt, and I (Ted) participated in our third book reading with a local school. Palma High is a private school for young men that partners with inmates at CTF to read and discuss various novels written by John Steinbeck. After discussing the reading about the book *Of Mice and Men* in small groups, participants would come together in a large group to share our discoveries. It was during one of these large group discussions where we began to catch a vision for an unprecedented mission.

Rob McLurg, a Palma guest and retired teacher shared a story from the book *Miracle on the River Kwai*. He explained how a small group of World War II POWs demonstrated a form of sacrificial love for their fellow man that inspired other prisoners to commit to a higher way of living. The prisoners' camp was populated by various allied forces, some of whom were Highlander Argylls from the British Army. It was custom among the Argylls for each man to have a *Mucker*, that is, someone with whom they would share their resources in order to ensure the friend for whom they were mucking would make it home alive. In the context of Mr. McLurg's share, Lenny and

Men Built For Others

George, the characters from *Of Mice and Men*, had been mucking for one another, which set them apart from most of the other ranch hands who lived as loners.

Already well into our efforts of collecting stories for this book, we took notice that what Mr. McLurg was sharing was a clear and compelling example of what it means to be a *Man Built for Others*.

Having since read the book *Miracle on the River Kwai*, the degradation of some of the POWs struck and resonated with me. The self-serving attitudes and scarcity mindset of the POWs were nearly identical to that of today's ordinary criminal prisoners. From the author's perspective, it was every man for himself in the POW camp, and their "me first" way of living created an atmosphere of despair where men gave up hope and lost their will to live. Similarly, this is the temptation that many prisoners and criminals alike face. Giving oneself over to this mentality is always a choice. However, if one is willing, he'll realize there are better alternative options available.

Angus McGillivray, one of the Highlander Argylls held captive on the River Kwai, made a different choice. When his *Mucker* became ill, and everyone believed he would die, Angus decided his *Mucker* would survive. Each day he'd draw his full ration and then stand over his friend to make sure that he finished it. When someone stole his *Mucker's* blanket, McGillivray gave him his own. He would often sneak out of camp at significant personal risk to barter for duck eggs that he would then give to his sick friend. Eventually, his *Mucker*, recovered, but the starvation and exhaustion took their toll on McGillivray, and he died.

Not only did McGillivray save his friends life, but his sacrifice also affected the entire camp. McGillivray's actions resulted in a higher ethical standard for the men. His behavior communicated: *This is the kind of men we were created to be. I believe this is how we're supposed to live. We need to stand in the gap for each other. We are supposed to love one another and be willing to lay down our own lives for our brothers.*

Nothing communicates values more clearly than action. And McGillivray's actions were so clearly evident that a fiery speech wasn't necessary. His self-sacrifice produced a transformational shift in attitude that eventually inspired the culture of the entire camp.

This powerful testimony reflects the spirit of a growing segment of the CTF population. While drawing comparisons between war heroes and criminals might seem odd, some inmates have committed taking a stand for something new. These men have chosen something other than living a life governed by limitations merely because they're in a prison culture that perpetuates a false message of "How it is." They have come to realize that what they've been doing has resulted in what they have been getting. Moreover, they understand that if they want something new, they will have to do something new. The men whose stories fill these pages are men who have committed their lives to something new. As a result of that commitment, they stand out amongst their peers. Their growth is by no means complete. However, their decision to honor their promises to serve their community raises the bar for the CTF community. Like McGillivray, they are most effective when their actions demonstrate how we are supposed to be living. When they are at their best, their choices and actions inspire and motivate those around them to a higher way of living.

Our collective experience has taught us that leaders are willing to go first. The men in this book prove that we can transcend the perceived and actual negativity of our circumstances and choose to live responsibly for ourselves and each other. Cumulatively, they've spent thousands of hours over the years facilitating small groups and mentoring other inmates who have shown interest in changing their lives. In this way, they have been our fellow workers in the effort to build rehabilitative programs and transform the culture of prison. We have been *Muckers* for each other and the CTF community at large.

When Mr. McLurg shared the story, I immediately thought of the men in our book as the CTF *Muckers*. But his account of the *Muckers* also planted a seed within our minds for whom we could become *Muckers* in the broader Salinas and Monterey community.

* * *

After spending time with the young men from Palma High over the course of three semesters, we were impressed by their character. Through our conversations, it became evident that they expected to attend excellent colleges. Many of them had received admission to schools like Notre Dame, UCLA, and Stanford. They have an incredible vision for their lives, and they will no doubt go on to accomplish amazing things. Their ambition seemed balanced by their humility and commitment to serving those less fortunate than themselves. For example, the students take trips to Mexico and Peru to build homes for people in need. They also tutor at-risk youth in Salinas.

With our experience of Palma's students and amazing faculty in mind, we decided that one of the best things we could do would be to provide a young man from Salinas with an opportunity to attend Palma High School. Realizing that such a commitment required more financial resources than we had access to as prisoners, we reached out to the Crop Organization, our long-time community partner. They loved the concept of a *Band of Muckers* coming together to provide a young man with a life-changing opportunity, and have since offered to help coordinate the outside fundraising campaign.

Following McGillivray's example, we knew that our actions would speak louder than our words. Therefore, we have committed one hundred percent of the profits from this book to the Crop Organization's *Men Built for Others'* scholarship fund.

Primary Contributor Profile

Name: Ted Gray
Date of Birth: 4/5/77
Sentence: 40 years-to-life
Parole Eligibility: 2023

Leadership Maxim: *Look at a man the way he is, and he only becomes worse. But look at a man as if he were what he could be, and he becomes what he should be.*
Person He Is Most Inspired By: His father, Mitch Gray
Favorite Book: *Season of Life* by Jeffrey Marx

Education & Interests
- Bachelor of Science in Health Care Administration
- Internationally Certified Alcohol and Drug Counselor II (ICADC-II)

TED GRAY is a founding member of Inside Solutions, a think tank of prosocial offenders who have committed themselves to transforming the culture of prison. Ted is at his best when he is building collaborative partnerships with outside organizations in order to provide authentic rehabilitative and leadership development opportunities. Ted is on the executive team of the Phoenix Alliance, a group that delivers transformational coaching and leadership development services to inmates as well as to students and faculty from local community colleges and high schools. Inspired by Joe Ehrmann's story from the *Season of Life*, Ted is currently working with his friends Richard Mireles, Jason Bryant, Matthew Braden, his Dad (Mitch Gray), and the Crop Organization to grow a culture of Men Built for Others.

Primary Contributor Profile

Name: Richard Mireles
Date of Birth: 11/30/77
Sentence: 25 years-to-life
Parole Eligibility: 2018

Leadership Maxim: *A man's gotta do what a man's gotta do.*
Person He Is Most Inspired By: His mother, Carmen
Favorite Book: *Soul Winner* by Charles H. Spurgeon

Education & Interests
- Bachelor of Science in Health Care Administration
- Internationally Certified Alcohol and Drug Counselor II (ICADC-II)

RICHARD MIRELES is a dynamic public speaker and expert communicator. In addition to being on the executive team of the Phoenix Alliance and a founding member of Inside Solutions, Rich is the only incarcerated associate trainer for John Maxwell's EQUIP Leadership and its *Million Leaders Mandate*. He is at his best when he is teaching the Bible, loving people, and inspiring people to be great in pursuit of a future worth having. He has been instrumental in training and coaching many of the leaders currently delivering rehabilitative programs at CTF-Soledad. Rich's highest commitment is to be a man of God, a good son, a good brother, a good friend, a good husband, and a man that his grandfather can be proud of. He looks forward to working with Ted, Jason, Matt, and the Crop Organization to grow the culture of Men Built for Others.

Primary Contributor Profile

Name: Jason Bryant
Date of Birth: 4/5/79
Sentence: 26 years-to-life
Parole Eligibility: 2023

Leadership Maxim: *Train your mind to create the good in every situation.*
Person He Is Most Inspired By: Barack Obama
Favorite Book: *Candide* by Voltaire

Education & Interests
- Master of Arts in Philosophy
- Bachelor of Arts in Business Administration
- *Internationally Certified Alcohol and Drug Counselor II* (ICADC-II)

JASON BRYANT is excited about life and enjoys meaningfully contributing to the health of communities. At his core, he is a philosopher who finds tremendous value in deep friendships and serving others through thoughtful conversations about new possibilities for their lives. He is a great listener with deep insights about how to help people get from where they are in life to where they could be. In addition to being a founding member of Inside Solutions, Jason is also on the executive team of the Phoenix Alliance. Jason's highest commitments are to strive to live virtuously and love the most important people in his life, his wife (Sandy), stepchildren (Celeste and David), and his mom (Jane).

Primary Contributor Profile

Name: Matthew Braden
Date of Birth: 3/21/76
Sentence: 28 years-to-life
Parole Eligibility: 2020

Leadership Maxim: *Don't wait for extraordinary opportunities; instead, seize common occasions and make them great.*
Person He Is Most Inspired By: Viktor Frankl
Favorite Book: *The Count of Monte Cristo* by Alexandre Dumas

Education & Interests
- Bachelor of Arts Degree in Sociology/Criminology (in progress)
- Six Associate's Degrees (in Arts and Science)
- Internationally Certified Alcohol and Drug Counselor II (ICADC-II)

MATTHEW BRADEN is epitomized by three words: efficient, tireless, and helpful. Matt is a dedicated leader who is not only on the executive team of the Phoenix Alliance, but he has also served on the Executive Body of multiple other self-help groups and acted as a lead counselor for the Crop Organization's Alcohol and Other Drug (AOD) program. Despite his many prison responsibilities and daily duties, Matthew's most endearing quality is that he is willing to put his work and responsibilities on hold in order to have conversations that matter with his peers. Whether they are seeking guidance about academic aspirations, looking for direction on how to prepare for parole, or simply wanting to talk about issues in their lives, Matt is always willing to lend his ear, his knowledge, and above all, his genuine concern for their well-being.

These pictures serve as great memories from one of our visits back in 2016 at the Correctional Training Facility (CTF) in Soledad, California.

If you'd like to learn more about the authors and contributors of *Men Built for Others*, please visit our website at www.menbuiltforothers.org

From left to right: Roger Nielsen, Richard Mireles, and Farshad Asl

From left to right: Roger Nielsen, Ted Gray, and Farshad Asl

CPSIA information can be obtained
at www.ICGtesting.com
Printed in the USA
FSHW020436220919
62201FS